ESSENTIAL JAPANESE

A Guidebook to Language and Culture

COMPILED BY LEXUS
*with Helmut Morsbach
and Kazue Kurebayashi*

*Japanese language consultant:
Anthony P. Newell*

PENGUIN BOOKS

PENGUIN BOOKS

Published by the Penguin Group
27 Wrights Lane, London W8 5TZ, England
Viking Penguin Inc., 40 West 23rd Street, New York, New York 10010, USA
Penguin Books Australia Ltd, Ringwood, Victoria, Australia
Penguin Books Canada Ltd, 2801 John Street, Markham, Ontario,
Canada L3R 1B4
Penguin Books (NZ) Ltd, 182–190 Wairau Road, Auckland 10, New Zealand

Penguin Books Ltd, Registered Offices: Harmondsworth, Middlesex, England

First published 1990
10 9 8 7 6 5 4 3 2 1

Filmset in Linotron Plantin Light
Made and printed in Great Britain by
Cox & Wyman Ltd, Reading

CONTENTS

INTRODUCTION

This is a guidebook to Japanese language and culture. Information is presented in one single A–Z listing in which dictionary and phrasebook elements are interwoven with descriptive passages on language, grammar and culture.

The dictionary/phrasebook elements give a vocabulary of some 1,500 everyday words and expressions, providing an excellent basis for self-expression in the foreign language.

The Japanese words and expressions are presented using the Roman alphabet so that they can easily be read out (in conjunction with the notes on pronunciation on page ix).

The language and grammar notes provide explanations of how the Japanese language works. If you want to go a little further, these sections will enable you to develop some basic skills with the Japanese language and to develop a knowledge of its structure.

More language notes and some useful expressions are given within the culture note entries: typical polite expressions, for example, what to say in specific circumstances, how to address your host etc. – all valuable language tips for the traveller.

The culture notes and cross-cultural comparisons cover a wide range of topics – from marriage to food, from public festivals to attitudes to handkerchiefs, from bathrooms to 'loss of face' – all having the same purpose of acting as a guide to a country that is not just foreign but different.

This book can operate at various levels. You can use it as a kind of travel book, to be read at home; you can take it abroad with you and use it as a dictionary/phrasebook; you can use it as an introduction to the Japanese language; or you can simply dip into it as a source of information about another civilization.

NOTES ON PRONUNCIATION

For more detailed comments on the pronunciation of Japanese see the entry PRONUNCIATION. The following points will help you read the translations in this book (very occasionally, where there is a potential problem, a pronunciation guide has also been given in square brackets after a translation in the text). But Japanese is very regular in its pronunciation and a few basic reminders will suffice. Vowel sounds are:

a	as in 'bath'
e	as in 'red'
i	like the i in 'Maria' but not quite as long
o	as in 'hot'
u	as in 'foot'
ai	as in 'Thailand'
ae	as if hyphenated a-eh
ei	as in 'weight'

A bar over a vowel means that the sound of the vowel is twice as long.

One very important point to remember is that Japanese does not have a silent 'e' as, for example, in the English word 'sake'. If 'sake' is read as a Japanese word then it is, of course, pronounced 'sa-ke'.

Consonants are largely as in English (bearing in mind the points made under PRONUNCIATION).

g	is always hard as in 'go' or 'girl'
y	is always as in 'you', never as in 'why'

Double consonants in Japanese (tt, nn etc.) should each be pronounced separately (like in Italian). Compare the difference between saying 'sure term' and 'short term'.

For an explanation of the bracketed words (no) and (na) see the entry ADJECTIVES.

For an explanation of the second verb form given between obliques (e.g. iku /ikimas/) see the entry VERBS.

A

A, AN
Japanese does not have articles, and no difference is usually made in the noun form between singular and plural. So, for example, the word **hito** can mean 'the person', 'a person', 'the persons', 'some persons', 'one person', 'persons', depending on context. For example:

> **can I have a cup of coffee?**
> kōhī o-negai shimas
> [*literally: coffee please*]

> **I want to hire a car**
> kuruma o karitai des
> [*literally: car (object) hire want is*]

about . . . (*concerning time*) . . . goro
  about 4 o'clock yoji goro
  (*all other measurements*) . . . gurai
  about two metres ni-mētoru gurai

above . . . (*preposition*) . . . no ue ni [no oo-eh nee]

accident (*traffic etc.*) jiko

adaptor (*for voltage changes*) adaptā

address jūsho
  what's the address? jūsho wa nan des ka?
  could you write the address down? jūsho o kaite kudasaimas ka?

ADDRESSES
In the Japanese (and Chinese) way of reasoning one moves from the periphery to the centre, addresses being no exception. Information which Westerners tend to give first or very soon is withheld to the last, like the verb in a Japanese sentence. An address on an envelope therefore starts with the most general information: postal area code, prefecture (province), city, followed by ward or section, and then the house number. Finally the addressee's name is added, with family name preceding the given name.
  For example:

Ṱ658	(postal code area)
Hyōgo-ken	(prefecture)
Kōbe-shi	(city)
Yamazaki-chō	(ward)

san-chōme	(section)
go-ban	(house number)
NAKADA Hiroshi	(family name, given name)
sama	(Mr/Mrs (very polite))

Westerners can write such addresses in Roman letters (called **rōma-ji**), either in the above order, or in the Western order. Care should be taken to print all letters clearly, since postal clerks may have trouble deciphering Westerners' handwriting.

ADDRESSING PEOPLE

There are several ways of addressing Japanese people.

Signs of respect

The most common is **-san**, which is roughly equivalent to Mr, Mrs or Miss and is added as a suffix to the name. The more polite version of **-san** is **-sama** (also a suffix) which is always used in the case of postal addresses (*see also* ADDRESSES).

-san and **-sama** should *never* be used after one's own name, since these words are a mark of respect from the speaker.

-san can be used after both given name and family name. For example, Mr James McKenzie could be either:

McKenzie-san

or:

James-san

Use of the given name and family name

In Japanese it is usual to use the surname, particularly in business and when speaking to people of higher rank. The given name (equivalent to our Christian name) is used almost exclusively with friends or family. (Note that the Japanese surname always comes before the given name when the full name is given, i.e. the order is the opposite of what we use in the West.)

If a person has a specific rank (e.g. Section Chief in a company), he is almost always addressed as **kachō** or **kachō-san** (or by whatever his rank is) by strangers and his subordinates. Alternatively the family name, followed by the person's title, is used. For example:

Nakada kachō – Section Chief Nakada

There are many other titles, for example **shachō** (president), **buchō** (head of division) etc. The same applies to teachers, doctors, dentists etc. or very senior persons who are addressed either as **sensei**, or by using family name plus **sensei**. For example:

Katō sensei – Professor Katō

sensei on its own is very useful if you have forgotten the name of the person you are speaking to in academic circles.

People in certain occupations can be addressed by their occupation (or name of shop) plus **-san**. For example:

o-mawari-san	Mr Policeman
denki-ya-san	Mr Electric Goods Store
niku-ya-san	Mr Butcher Shop

Children up to about ten years of age can be addressed by their given name, often abbreviated, with the suffix **-chan** (a diminutive of **-san**). Among each other, children switch from given name plus **-san** to family name plus **-san** when leaving high school and entering work or embarking on further study, or **-kun** if a senior is speaking to a junior male.

When both names are written, for example on a business card, the surname is written first. (On business cards the suffix **-san** is naturally omitted.) So for a Japanese whose given name is **Hiroshi** and whose surname is **Nakada** the correct order is:

Nakada Hiroshi-san (*when being addressed*)
Nakada Hiroshi (*on business cards*)

Since this is often written in Chinese-derived ideographs (**kanji**) only, it is quite in order to ask someone to spell his name for you and to write it on the card (*see* BUSINESS CARDS).

Some examples of addressing people are:

Greeting a person for the first time both privately and in business

kon-nichi wa, hajimemashte – Suzuki des – dōzo yoroshku
hello, how do you do? – I am Suzuki – pleased to meet you

Greeting older (or respected) people

kon-nichi wa, o-genki des ka?
hello, how are you?

Greeting a friend or younger person

kon-nichi wa, genki des ka?
hello, how are you?

Note that the word **genki** is directly translated as 'health' and has the honorific prefix **o** added to it to denote respect in the second of the last three examples.

Note also that in these examples **kon-nichi wa** has been used. This indicates that the time of day is between mid-morning and late afternoon. In the morning **ohayō (gozaimas)** would be substituted and in the evening **komban wa**.

See DIMINUTIVES

ADJECTIVES

Japanese 'adjectives' are a special category of words, many of which behave in a way quite unlike their English counterparts. Many, indeed, are more like verbs, since they have separate forms for present and past tenses and for positive and negative use. For example the word **akai**, which many books simply translate as 'red', actually means 'is-red'. And since it contains a verbal element, the word **akai** is, in effect, a perfectly grammatical one-word sentence. It is, however, a plain form (*see* PLAIN FORMS) so would not be used by itself in polite language at the end of a sentence – but adding **des** makes it polite:

> **is your car red?**
> anata no kuruma wa akai des ka?

The word **des** is not needed, however, if the adjective comes directly before its noun:

> **I need a red pen**
> akai pen ga irimas

Do not make the mistake of thinking that the word **des** means 'is' – it doesn't. It simply makes the sentence **akai** ('it is red') more polite. That's why it can also be used for sentences in the past form:

> **akakatta des**
> it was red

Again, **akakatta** by itself means 'it was red', but as it stands it is not a polite form.

These characteristics are shared by all adjectives having the following four endings: **-ai, -oi, -ui, ī** (= **ii**):

nagai	is long
omoshiroi	is interesting
warui	is bad
oishī	is delicious

The past and negative forms of these adjectives are formed as follows after removing the final -i from the present positive form:

present negative

naga	-ku nai	is not long
omoshiro	-ku nai	is not interesting
waru	-ku nai	is not bad
oishi	-ku nai	is not delicious

past positive

naga	-katta	was long
omoshiro	-katta	was interesting
waru	-katta	was bad
oishi	-katta	was delicious

Note that an **i** between **sh** and **k** usually disappears.

past negative

naga	-ku nakatta	was not long
omoshiro	-ku nakatta	was not interesting
waru	-ku nakatta	was not bad
oishi	-ku nakatta	was not delicious

These are all plain forms. To make them polite add **des** to all the positive forms. For the negative forms change:

nai to **arimasen**
nakatta to **arimasen deshta**

Here are some examples:

it's interesting, isn't it?
omoshiroi des ne?

it was really delicious
totemo oishkatta des

it's not bad (*polite form*)
waruku arimasen

All adjectives that don't have one of the four endings as given above (for example **kirei** – pretty, **shizuka** – quiet) are more like English adjectives. In the text of this book they are followed by (**na**) since the word **na** must be added if the adjective comes before a noun:

a quiet room
shizuka na heya

If such an adjective is used after a noun the **na** is dropped – but remember to add a verb since there is no verbal idea included as there is in the previous type of adjective:

heya wa shizuka des	the room is quiet
heya wa shizuka deshta	the room was quiet
heya wa shizuka ja arimasen	the room is not quiet

> **heya wa shizuka ja arimasen deshta**   the room was not quiet

The particle **no** is also used to form constructions parallel to English adjectives. When **no** is given in brackets in this book, follow the same rules as for **na**.

advance: in advance maemotte [mah-eh-motte]
advance payment maebarai [mah-eh-bah-ra-ee]

ADVERBS

To form adverbs from adjectives ending in **-ai, -oi, -ui, -ī** (= **ii**) change the final **-i** to **-ku**:

quick	hayai
quickly	hayaku
slow	osoi
slowly	osoku

To form adverbs from adjectives followed by (**na**) change **na** to **ni**:

> **shizuka na heya**
> a quiet room

> **shizuka ni hanasu**
> to speak quietly

advertisement kōkoku

aeroplane hikōki

after . . . . . . (no) ato de
after that (*then*) sore kara

If 'after' is used with a noun, the word **no** must be included:

> **after the festival**
> matsuri no ato de

> **after lunch**
> chūshoku no ato de

If it is used with a verb, however, the **no** disappears; the verb form to use is the 'plain past' (*see* PAST TENSE):

> **after eating, let's go to a film**
> tabeta ato de eiga ni ikimashō

> **I learned Japanese after going to Japan**
> Nihon e itta ato de Nihongo o naraimashta

after you dōzo o-saki ni

In Japan, males precede females, and seniors precede juniors. Problems can thus arise in the case of (fairly) high status Western females, who could collide with elderly Japanese gentlemen when passing through doors or entering/leaving lifts. **'Dōzo o-saki ni!'** said with a smile and a slight bow should lead to painless disentanglement.

afternoon gogo
    this afternoon kyō no gogo
    in the afternoon gogo ni
    good afternoon kon-nichi wa
There is no special post-lunch pre-dinner greeting in Japan. Approximate changeover time is before noon from **o-hayō gozaimas!** (good morning) to **kon-nichi wa** (good day). The next change is around 5 p.m. to **komban wa** (good evening).

aftershave aftā-shēbu

afterwards ato de

again mata

against ...... ni taishte
    to lean against the wall kabe ni motareru
    I'm against the idea kangae ni hantai des

agent (*in business*) dairi-nin

ago: a year ago ichi-nen mae [mah-eh]
    two months ago ni-kagetsu mae
    that was a long time ago sore wa daibu mae deshta

agree: I agree sansei shimas
    do you agree? (anata wa) sansei shimas ka?
    I don't agree sansei shimasen

agreement (*contract*) keiyaku

air kūki

air-conditioning reibō, kūrā

airline kōkūgaisha
    which airline is it? dono kōkūgaisha des ka?

airmail kōkūbin

airport kūkō　空港
    to the airport please kūkō made o-negai shimas

alcohol arukōru

ALCOHOL
Alcohol, especially rice wine or **sake** [sah-ke], has been part of Japanese culture since antiquity. It is estimated that half the entire population imbibes occasionally or often, especially during ceremonies, such as New Year celebrations, weddings, and funerals. During festivals, offerings are ritually

made to the deities. During the last century, Western alcoholic beverages have also become popular. For drinking customs *see* DRINK.

all: that's all, thanks ijō des, arigatō

One of the commonest words for 'all' is **zembu**, usually used after the noun:

> **all the hotels**
> hoteru zembu

> **all the money**
> o-kane zembu

The prefix **zen-** (**zem-** before a **-b**) is often found in compound words: **zenkoku** (all country), 'the whole country', **zentai** (all body), 'the whole lot'. But although **zen-** is a very common prefix meaning 'all', you can't just add it freely to anything. For 'all the people', 'all of us', 'all of them' (*everybody*) the word **mina** (more politely, **mina-san**) is often used:

> **how much would you charge for all of us?**
> mina de ikura deshō ka?

> **there are five of us in all**
> mina de go-nin des

almost hotondo

alone (*person*) hitori de
> **I'm travelling alone** (watakshi wa) hitori de ryokō shte imas

ALPHABET *see* WRITING SYSTEM

already sude ni

also . . . . . . mo
> **I'm also going** watakshi mo ikimas

although . . . . . . keredomo

This word *follows* verbs and adjectives:

> **although it's expensive**
> takai keredomo

> **although it's a rather expensive inn, it's very good**
> kono ryokan wa kanari takai keredomo, totemo ī des

In more polite speech, **des** can be added to adjectives:

> **although it's rather expensive, I'll buy it**
> kanari takai des keredomo, kaimas

Shorter, slightly less polite variants of **keredomo** are **keredo** and **kedo**.

altogether zembu
what does that make altogether? zembu de ikura des ka?

always itsumo
as always itsumo no yō ni

am *see* BE

America Amerika アメリカ

American (*adjective*) Amerika no
she's/he's American (kanojo/kare wa) Amerika-jin des
the Americans Amerika-jin

AND

Surprising though it may seem, such an apparently simple word as 'and' has all sorts of translations in Japanese; basically, however, we have to distinguish between 'and' with nouns and 'and' with verbs or adjectives. With nouns, we can simply use **to**:

> **beer and sake**
> bīru to sake

> **shrines and temples**
> jinja to o-tera

If we want to imply a longer list, we can use **toka** or **ya** in the following ways:

> **Americans and English people (among others)**
> Amerika-jin toka Igirisu-jin toka

> **I like peaches, persimmons, watermelons and things like that**
> momo ya kaki ya suika ga ski des

Note that where in English you can omit 'and' between nouns, in Japanese you can't.

However, the words **to**, **toka** and **ya** can *never* be used to link verbs, adjectives or sentences. Instead you have to use a particle form (*see* PARTICLES):

> **I drank too much and I've got a headache**
> sake o nomisugite, atama ga itai des

> **I'd like to go to the shrine and take some pictures**
> jinja e itte, shashin o toritai des

> **a room that's small and cheap**
> chīsakute yasui heya

> **a room that's quiet and cheap**
> shizuka de yasui heya

'And' at the beginning of sentence is **soshte**:

> **And the tickets are cheap**
> Soshte kippu wa yasui des yo

another: another beer, please bīru o mō ip-pai kudasai
> **another cup of coffee** kōhī o mō ip-pai
> **I'd like another room** (*a different one*) betsu no heya ga hoshī des

answer (*noun*) kotae [kota-e]
> **there was no answer** (*on telephone*) dare mo kotaemasen deshta

ANY

The word 'any' and its related family (anybody, anything, etc.) is another example of the difference between English and Japanese. For a start, the word 'any' is usually not translated at all:

> **did you buy any stamps?**
> kitte o kaimashta ka?

> **no, they didn't have any** (*stamps*)
> īe, kitte wa arimasen deshta

> **do you understand any English?**
> eigo ga wakarimas ka?

ANYBODY, ANYTHING, ANYWHERE

When it comes to related words like 'anybody', 'anything' or 'anywhere', we need to distinguish three types of sentence:

(a) positive questions

anybody	dareka
anything	nanika
anywhere	dokoka

For example:

> **did you buy anything?**
> nanika kaimashta ka?

> **did you meet anyone?**
> dareka ni aimashta ka?

(b) negative questions and statements

anybody	daremo
anything	nanimo
anywhere	dokonimo

For example:

> **isn't anyone coming?**
> daremo kimasen ka?

isn't it anywhere?
dokonimo arimasen ka?

I didn't buy anything
nanimo kaimasen deshta

(c) positive statements

anybody	daredemo
anything	nandemo
anywhere	dokodemo

For example:

anybody can do it
daredemo dekimas

anywhere will do
dokodemo ī des

I'll eat anything that tastes nice!
nandemo oishī mono o tabemas yo!

apology shazai
please accept our apologies sumimasen deshta (*see* SORRY)

approximately *see* **about**

April shi-gatsu

are *see* BE

arm ude [oo-de]

arrivals (*airport sign*) tōchaku

arrive tōchaku suru /tōchaku shimas/
he's arriving tomorrow (kare wa) ashta tōchaku shimas

ARTICLES *see* A, AN

ashtray haizara

Asia Ajia

ask kiku /kikimas/
I'll ask him kare ni kikimas
could you ask him? kare ni kīte kudasaimas ka?

asleep : be asleep nemutte iru /nemutte imas/
he's still asleep kare wa mada nemutte imas

assistant: my assistant watakshi no joshu

at: at my hotel watakshi no hoteru de
at the airport kūkō de
at 9 o'clock ku-ji ni

August hachi-gatsu

aunt (*own aunt*) oba
  (*someone else's*) oba-san

Australia Ōstoraria　オーストラリア

Australian (*adjective*) Ōstoraria no
  she's/he's Australian (kanojo/kare wa) Ōstoraria-jin
des
  the Australians Ōstoraria-jin

autumn aki [a-kee]
  in the autumn aki ni

average: on average heikin shte

B

back: my back senaka
  I'll be right back sugu modorimas
  when we go back home kaeru toki
  back home in England kuni no Igirisu dewa

bad (*person, deal*) warui
  (*food*) kusatta

bag (*made of paper*) kamibukuro
  (*made of cloth*) nunobukuro
  (*suitcase*) ryokōkaban, sūtsukēs

baggage nimotsu

ball-point pen bōru-pen

bamboo take

bank ginkō   銀行

bank account ginkō-kōza

bank loan ginkō-kashitske

bankrupt: to go bankrupt tōsan suru /tōsan shimas/
  bankrupt person tōsan-sha

BANKS
Unlike in Britain, cash dispensers are often located inside banks (and post offices), not outside, and thus tend to be unavailable when most urgently needed. However, since they are separated from the normal bank interior, they are open longer hours than the bank proper – approximately until 6 p.m. There are some exceptions in the centres of cities, where all-night cash facilities have recently become available. All this assumes that you have already become a customer of a Japanese bank, and were issued with its cash card.

bar (*drinks*) (*Western-style*) bā
  (*Japanese-style*) nomi-ya

bath o-furo
  public bath house sentō
  Turkish bath sōpu-rando

bathroom furo-ba

BATHS

In Japan the bath is more than a matter of cleanliness – it is a daily chance to relax and to cleanse both body and mind. Large Western-style hotels for businessmen naturally have bathtubs similar in function to the ones back home (only smaller).

In older times bathing in a poor country blessed with an abundance of water meant that people took turns (usually in the evening) using the same bathwater in a deep tub. Therefore, during the cleaning stage one squats outside the tub and cleans oneself thoroughly before enjoying (almost) total immersion, taking care not to dirty the water with soap etc. In public baths, where the sexes are segregated, there is a central pool holding a dozen or more bathers, while the others squat at the edge of the large room near the taps. Increasing affluence means that most Japanese families now have a bath at home. As a guest of honour you may be invited to be the first one in the evening to enter the bath. If the water is too hot, please check if you are permitted to add cold water. To do this ask:

mizu o irete mo ī des ka?

On entering, you may hear the host say:

dōzo go-yukkuri
please take your time

bathtub o-furo, yokusō

battery denchi, kan-denchi

bay wan
    Tokyo bay Tōkyō wan

BE

Whereas in English the single verb 'to be' has many uses, the Japanese language requires several different verbs. One important function of this is to make a clear distinction between living and non-living objects. If a living thing is located somewhere, the Japanese equivalent of 'to be' is:

iru (dictionary form) or **imas** (polite form).

Used as an independent verb, **iru** can only indicate location:

Mr Smith is in this room
Sumisu-san wa kono heya ni imas
[*literally: Smith Mr (subject) this room in is*]

If an inanimate object is located somewhere, 'to be' is:

aru (dictionary form) or **arimas** (polite form).

Mr Smith's bag is in this room
Sumisu-san no kaban wa kono heya ni arimas
[*literally: Smith Mr of bag (subject) this room in is*]

When the condition of something, or its quality, or number has to be described, the word **da** (dictionary form) is used, though mostly in its polite form **des**. For example:

this is my coffee
kore wa watakshi no kōhī des
[*literally: this (subject) I of coffee is*]

An important feature of these verbs (as of all Japanese verbs) is that there are no separate forms for 'am', 'are' or 'is'. So for example:

Igirisu-jin des

can mean either:

I am English
or: he is English
or: she is English
or: we are English

all depending on context.

Likewise:

Tōkyō ni imas

can mean:

I am in Tokyo
or: he is in Tokyo
or: they are in Tokyo etc.

and **Tōkyō ni arimas**

can mean:

it is in Tokyo
or: they are in Tokyo (*things*)

Let's now look at the negative and past forms of these three verbs, how to say 'was', 'were', 'wasn't' etc.

present positive	*present negative*
des	ja arimasen
imas	imasen
arimas	arimasen

past positive	*past negative*
deshta	ja arimasen deshta
imashta	imasen deshta

arimashta   **arimasen deshta**

And two examples:

he was in Tokyo last year
kyo-nen Tōkyō ni imashta

the containers weren't there
kontenā wa soko ni arimasen deshta

beard hige

beautiful (*woman*) utskushī
(*day*) sugoku ī
(*meal*) oishī

BECAUSE

This can be expressed by **kara** following a 'polite verb' (*see* VERBS):

he feels sleepy because he's drunk too much
sake o nomi-sugimashta kara nemuku nari-mashta

I'm not going today because I'm too busy
isogashī des kara, kyō wa ikimasen

'because of' can be translated by '**. . . no tame ni**' or just '**. . . de**':

I'm not buying it because of the price
nedan no tame ni kaimasen

it's closed because of the typhoon
taifū de shimatte imas

bed (*Western-style*) beddo
(*Japanese-style*) futon
I have to go to bed ne-nakereba narimasen
he's in bed (kare wa) nete imas

bedroom shin-shitsu

BEDS

Beds in Western-style hotels differ little from the ones you are used to at home. Welcome extras in your hotel room may be slippers, facilities for brewing Japanese tea, as well as a neatly folded **yukata** and **obi** (thin cotton gown with belt) which is used for nightwear. In summer you can even go for a stroll outside in it, provided you are in a resort hotel! Take care to fold the left part of the (button-less) **yukata** over the right before girding yourself with the **obi**. The opposite way, right over left, will only be used once – when you are a corpse at a wake, about to be buried.

Japanese-style beds or **futon** consist of pliable mattresses or **shki-buton** and thick quilts or **kake-buton** as well as pillows, **makura**. They are stored in cupboards during the day and spread out at night on the **tatami**-mat floor, thus allowing the room to be used for other purposes during the daytime. If you stay in a Japanese-style inn or **ryokan**, the maid will lay out your bed after you have had dinner in your room. But if you stay in a less expensive **minshuku** (people's inn), bedding has to be laid out and put away by yourself.

beef gyū-niku

beer bīru

    two beers, please bīru futatsu o-negai shimas

before . . . . . . (no) mae ni [ma-eh]

If 'before' is used with a noun, the word **no** must be included:

> **before Wednesday**
> sui-yōbi no mae ni

> **before the next meeting**
> tsugi no kaigi no mae ni

> **before the trip**
> ryokō no mae ni

If it is used with a verb, however, the **no** disappears; the verb form to use is the 'plain present' (*see* PLAIN FORMS):

> **before going to the film, let's eat**
> eiga o mi ni iku mae ni, tabemashō

> **I learned Japanese before I went to Japan**
> Nihon e iku mae ni, Nihongo o naraimashta

> **haven't we met before?**
> mae ni atta koto ga arimasen ka?

Strictly speaking, this expression should be used only when the speaker knows 'when' something is going to happen or has some control over it (in the above examples, 'eating' or 'going to Japan'). But in the case of, say, forgetting something or the weather turning bad, *when* it will happen is not clear, and is uncontrolled. In such cases, a negative plain present is used with **uchi ni**:

> **before I forget**
> wasurenai uchi ni

> **let's go home before it rains**
> ame ga furanai uchi ni kaerimashō

begin (*transitive*) hajimeru /hajimemas/
(*intransitive*) hajimaru /hajimarimas/
let's begin! hajimemashō!

BEHAVIOUR

Japanese behaviour can change dramatically, depending on circumstances. In polite society, and with strangers (including Westerners), Japanese behaviour tends to be highly restrained and self-conscious. A pity that most Westerners never get to see really relaxed behaviour, apart from the alcohol-induced variety!

Although the slurping sound when drinking fluids (and when eating noodles) is quite common even in 'polite' settings, yawning will be suppressed, as will be blowing one's nose, belching and farting. In a thoroughly familiar setting, however, these bodily expressions are far less tabooed than in the West.

behind ... (*spatially*) ... no ushiro ni
(*in time*) ... okurete
behind schedule yotei o okurete

believe shinjiru /shinjimas/
he'll never believe it kare wa, keshte sore o shinjinai deshō

below ... (*spatially*) ... no shta ni
(*in amount*) ... ika

best (*product etc.*) mottomo yoi
we'll do our best saizen o tsukushimas

better yori yoi
that's better sore hō ga ī des

between ...... no aida ni

bid (*noun*) tsuke-ne

big ōkī

bill o-kanjō
can I have the bill, please? o-kanjō o o-negai shimas

bill of exchange tegata

BILLS

In Japan, paying money is treated like sex: discreetly. Whether buying or selling in Japan, your business partners will tend to invite you out and then pick up the tab themselves, since you are a guest in their country. You should therefore try to reciprocate when they visit your country in return. Naturally, you can also extend a return invitation and take them to a Western-style restaurant, where you know the menu and the prices.

Except among good friends or college students it is unusual to go Dutch. However, during informal drinking the suggestion may be made:

warikan de nomimashō ka?

in which case everyone pays separately and the bill is usually split evenly, rather than calculating individual consumption. If you want to pay, say:

watakshi ga haraimas!
I'll pay!

This could lead to a small struggle at the till, since the other(s) might insist on that privilege as well. Bills and change in reputable places are not scrutinized – to do so would show lack of trust in the establishment. There is very little cheating at this level, except for overpriced hostess bars which tend to pad your bills with enormous sums for tiny bowls of peanuts.

birthday tanjōbi
   happy birthday! o-tanjōbi omedetō (gozaimas)!

BIRTHDAYS

The only birthday traditionally celebrated in Japan is the baby's very first one, although Western customs (and greater individualism) now tend to call for a birthday cake with candles for older children as well. The custom of birthday presents is not yet widespread, though no doubt the ubiquitous Japanese business establishment is trying its best to propagate this.

In the past in Japan everyone became one year older on New Year's Day, which (among other things) made this the most auspicious day in the Japanese calendar. Another important birthday is one's sixtieth (when the Chinese-derived calendar has turned full circle, so that one starts one's retirement in child-like innocence). Finally, an eighty-eighth birthday is a cause for extensive celebration. This is due to the fact that the number '88', written in a special way with Chinese ideographs, also means 'rice', which has traditionally been revered in Japan.

biscuit bisketto

bit skoshi
    a little bit hon no skoshi
    a bit better mae yori (mo) ī des
    a bit of chocolate skoshi chokorēto

black kuroi

blanket mōfu

bless you!
    Sneezing calls for no comment from bystanders in
    Japan.

blood ketsu-eki

blood group ketsu-eki-gata

blue aoi [ah-oy]
    Japanese do not distinguish strictly between blue
    and green, as evidenced by the fact that traffic lights
    switch from red (**aka**) to **ao**.

board of directors jūyaku-kaigi

boat (*small*) bōto
    (*ship*) fune
    by boat fune de

body karada

boiled egg yude tamago

boiled rice (*served in a bowl, with Japanese food*) gohan
    (*served on a plate with Western food*) raisu

book (*noun*) hon

borrow kariru /karimas/

boss (*formal word*) jōshi
    (*informal word*) boss
    my boss watakshi no jōshi

both (*things*) ryōhō
    I'll buy both of them ryōhō o kaimas
    (*people*) futari-tomo
    I met both of them futari-tomo ni aimashta
    both . . . and . . . . . . mo . . . mo
    I saw both Mr Kimura and Mr Yasunaga
    Kimura-san mo Yasunaga-san mo mimashta

bottle bin

bottle-opener sen-nuki

bottom (*of box etc.*) soko

box hako

boy shōnen, otoko-no-ko (*less formal*)

bra buraj'yā

brake (*noun*) burēki

branch (*of company*) shten

brand image shōhin imēji

brandy burandei

breach: a breach of contract keiyaku ihan

bread pan パン
　could I have some bread, please? pan o kudasaimas ka?

breakfast asa-gohan

BREAKFAST

These days between the hours of 6 and 8 a.m. about half of all Japanese households have Western-style breakfast. This is quicker to make than the traditional cooking of rice etc., and consists of cereals, toast, coffee and fried eggs. Japanese-style breakfast consists of rice with a raw egg stirred in, **miso** soup (made from soy beans), seaweed (**nori**), sticky beans (**nattō**) and pickle (**tsukemono**). Good for your health – give it a try! Some hotels and most Japanese-style inns (**ryokan**) offer you a choice. Better still, give it several tries and suspend your judgement (as with so many other Japanese things) until you have become better acquainted with it.

bridge hashi

briefcase shorui-kaban

bring motte kuru /motte kimas/
　I didn't bring it with me sore o motte kimasen deshta

Britain Igirisu イギリス
Literally this means 'England'. You can also use the word **Eikoku**, which means 'Britain'. 英国

British Igirisu no (*or* Eikoku no)
　I'm British Igirisu-jin des (*or* Eikoku-jin des)

brochure pamfretto
　our company brochure watakshi-tachi no kaisha-pamfretto

broken (*arm etc.*) kossetsu-shta
　(*calculator etc.*) kowareta

brother (*general*) kyōdai
　(*older, talking about one's own*) ani

(*older, someone else's*) o-nī-san
(*younger, talking about one's own*) otōto
(*younger, someone else's*) otōto-san

BROTHERS

Rank and order of birth remain vitally important in present-day Japan, so that there is as yet no general term for 'brother'. Even in the case of identical twins, one is usually regarded as the senior one (for life) simply by beating his/her sibling to the outside world by a few minutes. However, in some parts of Japan it is the latter-born who is regarded as 'senior', since he/she has already occupied a higher position in his mother's womb for nine months.

The younger brother has to call his older brother **o-nī-san** for life (in the case of older sisters **o-nē-san**), while junior is called by his/her first name only, without title, in return.

Traditionally, the eldest son or **chōnan** had the responsibility of staying at home and looking after his parents, allowing the younger ones to get a good education as part of their inheritance, and to set out on their own.

brown cha-iro

Buddha hotoke
(*polite form*) hotoke-sama

Buddhism buk-kyō

budget (*noun*) yosan

building tatemono

bullet train shinkan-sen

bus basu
  by bus basu de

bus station basu no tāminaru

bus stop basu no バスの停留所

business (*company*) kaisha
  company business shayō
  I'm here on business shigoto de koko ni imas
  it's a pleasure to do business with you shigoto ga dekite ureshī des
  we look forward to a fruitful business relationship o-tagai ni shigoto ga umaku iku to ī des nē
  business is business! shigoto wa shigoto!

BUSINESS

One major difference between Japanese and Western ways of doing business is the greater stress placed in Japan on long-lasting personal relations (*see* FAMILY), which take much time and effort to set up. Quick profits are of minor concern. Cultural factors are therefore of great importance, since business partners must find one another sympathetic before negotiations have a hope of succeeding. A lot of wining and dining and exchanging of gifts may therefore be needed to establish and to cement ties. Discussions (usually arranged through go-betweens trusted by both parties) may take a very long time, but once decisions have been reached they are usually implemented with speed. One must be prepared to work long hours with little thought of 'this is not my business' or 'now I am off duty'.

Knowledge of Japanese culture and language can be of help, showing your willingness to learn more about your partner. While almost all of your business discussion will be in English, your knowledge of Japanese language and culture should include greetings, pleasantries, and a knowledge of how to avoid major mistakes.

business card meishi

BUSINESS CARDS

A business card is of vital importance in Japan when introductions are made, especially in business circles. Those Japanese frequently dealing with foreigners will have the information in Japanese on one side of the card and in English on the reverse. The Japanese sequence is usually: name of company, one's status in it (e.g. 'Section Chief, Export Division'), family name and then first name. This is followed (in small writing) by the company's address and phone number. Among businessmen, the home address is usually not given.

Take care to have your own name correctly transcribed into Japanese, ideally before departure from your home country. Your address (in the West) need not be translated, since it is available on the English side. This changes if you reside in Japan for a length of time.

Avoid garish or over-complicated business cards – there is no need for product descriptions, etc.

On introduction, bow (or shake hands), then get a **meishi** from your wallet and hand it over, English side topmost (otherwise it may imply that your partner doesn't understand English), and in such a way that it can be read without having to be turned around. Read your partner's **meishi** carefully, and ask for the correct pronunciation of the family name if this is not clear (sometimes a **meishi** is in Japanese writing only). After sitting down to talk, you can keep the one (or several) **meishi** received in front of you on the table, or on the armrest of your chair, checking it when necessary. Finally, put the **meishi** away carefully – on no account treat it lightly, e.g. by dumping it in an ashtray! Nor should you pass it on casually to a subordinate of yours. Afterwards you might like to collect all the important **meishi** in a special 'meishi album' which can be bought at Japanese stationery shops or **bumbōgu-ya**, so that you can keep track of all the names when meeting next.

business hotel bijines hoteru

BUSINESS HOTELS
These have fewer frills than international hotels, but are considerably cheaper. Rooms (usually Western-style) are small, and the attached bathroom/toilet is often a useful practice area for circus contortionists. However, they are clean, though you might have trouble making yourself understood in English. For reasons of your firm's prestige (very important in Japan) you might be obliged to stay in a high-class hotel. Check with travel agents back home – sometimes luxury hotels can be booked as part of an all-inclusive package.

business trip shutchō

businessman kaisha-in

businesswoman joshi sha-in, bijines ūman

busy (*person*) isogashī
(*streets*) nigiyaka (na)
(*telephone line*) o-hanashi-chū

BUT
There are many ways of translating 'but', one of the commonest being **ga**, which combines two sentences expressing a contrast:

> **I drink beer but I don't drink sake**
> bīru wa nomimas ga, sake wa nomimasen

I'd like to go but I have no money
ikitai to omoimas ga, o-kane ga arimasen

The second part of the sentence is sometimes omitted since it is often understandable from the context, or perhaps the speaker wishes to imply something without actually saying it. It is typical of a Japanese speaker to leave the listener in suspense as to *exactly* what is meant. It is the listener's job to infer, and not force the speaker to be too explicit, especially if what is being said has some sort of negative force:

the room's quiet but . . . (I don't really like it)
heya wa shizuka des ga . . .

However, it should be noted that this **ga** may also be added to the end of a sentence as a kind of 'softener', just making things seem less definite. It needn't always imply a negative follow-on.

Note also that **ga** cannot be used at the beginning of a sentence. For that, use **demo**, **dakedo** or **shkashi**:

but what about your husband?
demo, go-shujin wa?

but my second son is still at school
shkashi, jinan wa mada seito des

You may hear several other phrases meaning 'but', including phrases like **de naku** or **dewa nakute**:

not in London but over here
Rondon de naku, koko des

butter batā

button botan

buy kau /kaimas/

by: by train densha de
by plane hikōki de
by what time? nan-ji made ni?
by 9.30 ku-ji-han made ni
by Friday kin-yōbi made ni
See PASSIVE VERBS

C

café kissaten

CAFÉS

Lack of privacy at home means that many meetings take place in coffee shops, of which there is a bewildering variety. For the price of one (expensive) coffee, you can stay as long as you like, getting endless servings of free ice-water. The price of the cheapest item (about two pounds) is thus a kind of admission ticket for a lengthy sojourn. You can discuss business there, meet friends, listen to jazz or classical music, be tortured by muzak, or look at beautiful waitresses in especially expensive **bijin kissaten** (beauty **kissaten**). In **dōhan kissaten** (together-er **kissaten**), often situated one floor above the regular shop, you can be so private with your coffee and your partner that the rest of the world doesn't know (or care?) for a time what you are up to . . .

Paradox: while Japanese tea is mostly served free, and without being asked for (e.g. when visiting a firm), Western-style coffee and Western-style tea are very expensive, thus to be sipped slowly and appreciatively. Yes, there are also coffee shops specializing only in coffee – ten, twenty, thirty varieties, in a tiny place, seating maybe five or six persons. Finding 'your' coffee shop (which has a public phone for your convenience) is important, as it is for a Frenchman living in Paris. On leaving a pleasant coffee shop, ask for their **matchi** (match box) with name, address and phone number at the counter, so that you can find the place again.

cake kēki

calculator keisanki

calendar karendā
See DATES

call: what's it called? sore wa nan to īmas ka?
    can I make a call to London? Rondon ni denwa o suru koto ga dekimas ka?
    I'll call back later (*on phone*) ato de denwa shimas

calligraphy shodō

camera kamera

CAN

When 'can' refers to ability rather than permission, the simplest phrase is 'plain present' verb (*see* PLAIN FORMS) plus the expression **koto ga dekiru (dekimas):**

can you repair it?
naosu koto ga dekimas ka?

you can get to Kyōto in two hours
Kyōto made ni-jikan de iku koto ga dekimas

Commoner, perhaps, though more difficult for the foreigner, is the use of the 'potential' form of the verb:

can you speak English?
eigo ga hanasemas ka?

can you eat sushi?
sushi ga taberaremas ka?

When 'can' is used in requesting permission, use the 'participle form' of the verb (*see* PARTICLE) plus the phrase **mo ī des ka?** (literally, 'is it good to . . .?', 'is it OK to . . .?'):

can I shut the window?
mado o shimete mo ī des ka?

can I take a photo?
shashin o totte mo ī des ka?

Here are some more useful phrases using the word 'can':

I can't speak Japanese
Nihongo ga dekimasen

we can supply them in six months
rok-kagetsu de sorera o kyōkyū dekimas

can we have a little more time?
mō skoshi jikan ga arimas ka?

can you put that in writing?
sore o kaite kudasaimas ka?

where can I find . . .?
. . . wa doko ni arimas ka?

For 'cannot' in the sense of prohibition *see* **must.**

Canada Kanada カナダ

cancel torikesu /torikeshimas/
can I cancel it? sore o tori-keshte mo ī des ka?

capital (*money*) shihon-kin

capital city shuto

car kuruma
  by car kuruma de

car hire rentakā　レンタカー

car park chūshajō

card (*business*) meishi
  See BUSINESS CARDS

care of . . . . . . kata
  Mr Smith, care of Mr Yamada Yamada-sama kata,
  Sumisu-sama

carpet kāpetto

case (*suitcase*) ryokōkaban, sūtsukēs

cash (*money*) genkin
  can you cash this cheque for me? kono kogitte o
  genkin ni dekimas ka?

cassette kasetto

cassette recorder kasetto rekōdā

catch: I'll catch the next train tsugi no densha ni
  norimas
  where do I catch a bus for . . .? . . . yuki no basu
  niwa, doko de noremas ka?

central heating chūō-dambō-sōchi

centre chūō

chair isu

chairman (*of company*) kaichō
  (*of meeting*) gichō

change: can I change some money? o-kane o ryōgae
  dekimas ka?
  could you give me some small change for this? kore
  o ko-zeni ni shte kudasaimas ka?
  do I have to change trains? densha o norikae-
  nakereba ikemasen ka?
  I'd like to change my flight bin o kaetai no des [kah-
  eh-tie]
  we've made some changes to the design dezain o
  ikuraka henkō shimashta

character (*written*) kanji
  See WRITING SYSTEM

cheap yasui
  it's cheap sore wa yasui des

check: I'll check it sore o shirabemas
  could you please check that? sore o shirabete
kudasaimas ka?

cheerio de wa mata
  (*more informally*) ja ne

cheers (*toast*) kampai!
  See TOASTS

cheese chīzu

chemist's kusuri-ya　薬屋

cheque kogitte
  can I pay by cheque? kogitte de haraemas ka?

cheque-book kogitte-chō

cheque card
  These are not used in Japan.

CHEQUES
Apart from in big business, cheques are little used in
Japan for daily transactions. Cash is still enormously
popular, but credit cards are gaining ground.

cherry blossom sakura

chest (*of body*) mune
  (*container*) hako

chicken (*food*) toriniku, chikin
  (*animal*) niwa-tori

children kodomo

baby	akachan (*or* akambō)
girl	onna-no-ko
boy	otoko-no-ko
daughter	musume
son	musuko
oldest daughter	chōjo
oldest son	chōnan

CHILDREN
If you are invited to a Japanese home, you might
like to take a present for the children. This is a must
between 1 and 15 January, when New Year visits are
in full swing. In that case, having ascertained how
many children there are, get a special envelope from
a stationery shop (**bumbōgu-ya**) for the money gift

called **otoshi-dama** and insert new bills to the value of 2,000-3,000 Yen into each one.

Since olden times it has been a colourful custom for all girls aged five, and all boys aged three and seven, to pay a visit to the nearest shrine on 15 November with their family to celebrate **shichi-go-san** (seven-five-three) – a marvellous day to see children's kimono.

Child-rearing is primarily the wife's responsibility, all the more so since the average businessman has to get up before his children are awake and only gets home after the children have gone to bed. Child-rearing is taken very seriously by mothers, and is achieved by giving in to the small child's wishes for the first four to five years, then applying achievement-oriented pressure year by year. Children are therefore more dependent than in the West, and, on the whole, very well behaved. Childhood is a 'Paradise Lost' for most grown-up Japanese, so one could argue that their drinking sessions, etc. are an attempt to return to it, however brief it may be. Childlike amusements among businessmen in the after-hours may seem pleasant or boring to you, depending on your own attitude, but if you accuse Japanese adults of 'childlike' or even 'childish' behaviour on occasion, remember that their behaviour in Japan is regarded as 'normal': from that viewpoint Westerners often seem 'uptight' by comparison. Enjoy the many simple, childlike pleasures (e.g. bathing, eating, drinking) which Japanese culture has to offer!

China Chūgoku

Chinese (*adjective*) Chūgoku no
(*person*) Chūgoku-jin

chips poteto furai

chocolate chokorēto

chopstick rest hashi-oki

chopsticks hashi
(*if joined together before use, and disposable*) waribashi
See EATING HABITS

Christian name namae

CHRISTIAN NAMES
Since very few Japanese are Christians, this name can be misleading. It may be better to use the term

'given name'. By law, Japanese can only have one given name, which is always placed after the family name. Mr Ken H. Yamamoto thus identifies himself as a non-Japanese (probably American) citizen. Given names are chosen for all kinds of auspicious reasons and can be very complicated and hard to pronounce when one sees only the **kanji** (ideographs). It is therefore quite in order to ask your partner on first meeting how his/her name is pronounced (*see* BUSINESS CARDS). Remember, however, not to use this given name unless you become very good friends. Family name and **-san** should be used instead. If you do use the given name, remember to use the word **-san** after it. For example:

hello, Keiko
Keiko-san, kon-nichi wa

Christianity kirisuto-kyō

CHRISTIANITY
Much of Christian teaching, emphasizing the individual's relation to an all-powerful God, differs drastically from traditional Japanese ways of thinking and behaviour. In spite of many decades of missionary activity, Christians number no more than one per cent of the total population. Christians have contributed much to education and hospital services, but on the whole their influence is not large. However, there is complete religious freedom in Japan.

Christmas kurisumas

CHRISTMAS
Owing to the relative absence of Japanese Christians, Christmas in Japan can be a wholly business-inspired commercial festival, with jingle bells and Father Christmases, uncontaminated by any other-worldly ideas. It helps that Christmas is close to the end of the year, when the Japanese traditionally get a bonus of two months' salary or more, so that there is often money to burn. Furthermore, end-of-the-year parties are common during this time, so that Christmas, although not a national holiday, can be celebrated with much merriment. Christmas presents, however, are not customary – but presents are

exchanged instead during the last days of December
as **o-seibo** (end-of-year gifts).

church kyōkai

CHURCHES
While Christians ought to go to church regularly,
the Japanese, who are mostly adherents of **Shintō** as
well as Buddhism, go to their shrine and temple on
festival days only, e.g. for **shichi-go-san** (*see* CHIL-
DREN). There are no sermons – only brief prayers for
good luck after tossing a coin into a receptacle at the
entrance, clapping of hands, and bowing. Real
religious feeling is shown by families who keep a
butsudan (house altar) where the spirits of the house
ancestors are venerated. This custom is said to be
increasing, even among present-day flat-dwellers, in
spite of the fact that they have little space to spare
for a **butsudan**.

cigar hamaki

cigarette tabako

cine-camera eigayō-kamera

cinema eigakan

city machi

city centre machi no chūshin

clean (*adjective*) kirei (na)

clock tokei

closed (*shop etc.*) heiten
(*box etc.*) shimatte iru

clothes (*Western-style*) yōfuku
(*Japanese-style*) wafuku, kimono

CLOTHES
For everyday wear, Japanese don Western-style
clothes to work. Here, dress seems to be more formal
than in the West, even in the sticky-hot summer
months – dark suits, white shirts, ties (*see* FORMAL-
ITY). Females must wear stockings at all times when
working in business, although there are knee-length
nylon stockings for the very hot days.
   Tall Westerners might have trouble buying suitable clothes. They should also avoid dressing in a
flashy way. The pink shirt of a junior official in the

British Embassy once caused some astonishment since only quiet colours should be worn for work.

However, and especially in summer, loose cotton gowns or **yukata** are worn at home, in Japanese-style hotels and outside at **onsen** (spas). These buttonless gowns, tied around the waist by an **obi** (sash), are the same for both sexes (*see* BEDS).

Traditional **kimono** are worn by women only rarely – they can best be seen during the New Year celebrations, for weddings and for graduation ceremonies. Men wear their traditional **kimono** (called **hakama**) even more rarely, though some slight revival may be taking place nowadays.
See SHOES

coat (*overcoat*) kōto

code (*dialling*) shigai kyokuban

coffee kōhī
 white coffee miruku kōhī
 black coffee burakku kōhī

COFFEE

Coffee is very expensive in Japan, especially at coffee shops (*see* CAFÉS). The normal drink is green tea, served all time of the day and drunk without any additions, such as milk or sugar.

coin: a ten-Yen coin jū-en-dama
 a hundred-Yen coin hyaku-en-dama

COINS

Owing to the recent introduction of value-added tax you will get quite a lot of one-Yen coins as change for most purchases, even when buying postage stamps and food items.

Five-Yen coins (relatively rare) have a hole in the centre and one is often kept in the wallet for good luck, since **go-en** ('five Yen') also means 'a good relationship with money', i.e. 'prosperity'.

Ten-Yen coins are most important, since local phone calls cost that little, making possible several minutes of non-stop talking and bowing to an invisible partner.

Fifty-Yen coins again have a hole in the centre and are silver-coloured.

Hundred-Yen coins are useful for **bending mashin** (vending machines).

Since 500-Yen coins have not been around for many years, quite a few vending machines do not yet accept them (*see also* MONEY).

cold (*weather etc.*) samui
　(*water, food etc.*) tsumetai
　it's cold (*weather*) samui des
　I've got a cold kaze o hīte imas
　cold water (*in restaurant*) o-hiya

COLDS
Since the First World War's flu epidemic, gauze masks called **masku** worn over mouth and nose have become popular in Japan when one has a cold. While (seemingly endless) sniffling is permitted, loud blowing of one's nose in a handkerchief is not. Should you have a cold, try to wipe your nose silently and discreetly with tissues.

colour iro

colour film karā firumu

comb (*noun*) kushi

come kuru /kimas/
　he's coming tomorrow (kare wa) ashta kimas
　I come from . . . . . . kara kimashta
　when are you coming to England? itsu Igirisu ni kimas ka?

comic manga

committed: we are committed to the project kono keikaku o jikkō shimas

company (*business*) kaisha

COMPARISON OF ADJECTIVES
Japanese adjectives do not have special forms to indicate comparison. However, the words **motto** (more) and **mottomo** (most) can be placed before an adjective to give the idea of comparison; likewise one can use the word **ichiban** (number one). For example:

　ichiban oishī
　the tastiest (dish)
　[*literally: number one delicious*]
　motto omoshiroi hon
　a more interesting book
　mottomo omoshiroi hon
　the most interesting book

motto hayaku
faster

ichiban benri na hoteru
the most convenient hotel

If you want to say, 'X is quicker than Y', the pattern to be used is:

X wa Y yori hayai des
[*literally: X (subject) Y more than quick is*]

For example:

trains are quicker than taxis
densha wa takshī yori hayai des
[*literally: train(s) (subject) taxi(s) compared to* quick is/are]

Examples of superlatives:

bananas are the cheapest
banana wa mottomo yasui des
[*literally: banana(s) (subject) most cheap is/are*]

or:

banana wa ichiban yasui des
[*literally: banana(s) (subject) number one cheap is/are*]

competitive kyōsōryoku (na)

complaint (*formal*) fuhei
(*informal*) monku

computer kompyūtā

conditions (*of contract*) keiyaku jōken

conference kaigi

conference room (*in hotel etc.*) kaigi-shitsu

consignment (*of goods*) itaku-hambai-hin

constipation bempi

consul ryōji
the British consul Igirisu (Eikoku) ryōji

contact: I'll get in contact with him kare ni renraku shimas
where can I contact you? doko de renraku dekimas ka?

contact lenses kontakto renzu

container (*for shipping*) kontenā
(*for food*) yōki

contract (*noun*) keiyaku

cool (*weather*) suzushī

corkscrew sen-nuki

corner (*of street*) kado
(*in room*) sumi
at the corner kado ni
in the corner sumi ni

correct (*adjective*) tadashī
that's correct sore wa tadashī des
(*it's as you say*) sono tōri des

cost (*noun*) genka
what does it cost? sore wa ikura des ka?
let's look at the costs genka o mite mimashō
the cost of ...... no genka

cotton wool dash-shimen

could: could I ...? ... (*participle*) mo ī des ka?
could you ...? ... (*participle*) kudasaimas ka?
could I open the window? mado o akete mo ī des ka?
could you write it down for me? sore o kaite kudasaimas ka?

COUNTING OBJECTS

This is very complex in Japanese, since several systems are used, depending on context. For example, if we want to say, 'I see two or three X', the way of saying this depends on the nature of the objects concerned. A different number word or 'counter' will be used according to the objects being counted. For example:

three friends came (*person counter:* **nin**)
tomodachi san-nin ga kimashta
[*literally: friend(s) three (subject) came*]

three books came (*book counter:* **satsu**)
hon san-satsu ga kimashta
[*literally: book(s) three (subject) came*]

two bottles of beer came (*counter for cylindrical objects:* **hon**)
bīru ni-hon ga kimashta
[*literally: beer(s) two (subject) came*]

three buses came (*counter for vehicles:* **dai**)
basu san-dai ga kimashta
[*literally: bus(es) three (subject) came*]

three bills came (*counter for flat objects:* **mai**)
kanjō san-mai ga kimashta
[*literally: bill(s) three (subject) came*]

Something similar (though much simpler) is found in English with phrases such as 'two sheets of paper', 'three rolls of film' etc.

However, for beginners it is only necessary to know two systems to make oneself understood:

	Japanese form		*Chinese-derived form*
1	**hitotsu**	一	**ichi**
2	**futatsu**	二	**ni**
3	**mittsu**	三	**san**
4	**yottsu**	四	**shi** (*or* **yon**)
5	**itsutsu**	五	**go**
6	**muttsu**	六	**roku**
7	**nanatsu**	七	**shichi** (*or* **nana**)
8	**yattsu**	八	**hachi**
9	**kokonotsu**	九	**kyū** (*or* **ku**)
10	**tō**	十	**jū**

Beyond this, only the Chinese numerals are used, e.g.:

11	**jū-ichi**	十一
12	**jū-ni**	十二
20	**ni-jū**	二十
33	**san-jū-san**	三十三
100	**hyaku**	百
1,000	**sen**	千
10,000	**ichi-man**	一万

55,555 would thus be:

go-man go-sen go-hyaku go-jū-go

五万五千五百五十五

Examples:

four coffees
kōhī yottsu

six apples
ringo muttsu

Note that the number word comes after the noun it is used with.

While the Chinese-derived word for four is **shi**, it is often replaced by **yon**, since **shi** also means 'death'. Thus there is no fourth floor in Japanese hospitals, neither is there a room 4 or room 44; one does not give presents (e.g. flowers or dishes) in sets of four, and unsuspecting foreign residents are often landed with telephone numbers containing many fours.

Westerners must take care once they get into large numbers, especially in money matters, since the highest denomination in bills (10,000 Yen) is not called **jū-sen-en** (ten thousand Yen) but **ichi-man-en** (one ten-thousand Yen) and thus may be written 1,0000. **ni-jū-man en** would thus be 'twenty ten-thousand Yen', i.e. 20,0000.

country (*nation*) kuni

couple: a couple of . . . ni-san no . . .

course: of course! mochiron!

crazy kichigai (no)
  that's crazy (sore wa) kichigai-zata des

cream (*for face, food, coffee*) kurīmu

credit card kurejitto kādo
  I've lost my credit cards kurejitto kādo o nakushte shimai-mashta

CREDIT CARDS
Credit cards have become very popular in Japan during recent years, and their use is similar to that in the West.

crisis kiki

crisps poteto chippsu

crowd hito-gomi

crowded konda

cultural exchange bunka kōryū

cup koppu
  a cup of green tea o-cha ippai
  a cup of black tea kō-cha ippai

cushion (*Western-style*) kusshon
  (*Japanese-style*) zabuton

CUSHIONS
Zabuton are spread on straw mats called **tatami**, usually round a low table. The proper way to sit on them is with one's stockinged or naked feet (never with shoes or slippers!) under the body, one big toe over the other. However, since this is painful for many (and not only for Westerners), cross-legged sitting is permitted for males. Western females can first sit down on the **zabuton** with their folded legs and feet underneath their body, and then slide off the feet slightly to one side. Erudite demonstrations of **ikebana** (flower arrangement) or **chanoyu** (tea

ceremony) are mostly remembered by Westerners for the agony caused by having had to remain motionless in this position while pretending to be appreciative.

custom shūkan
  a Japanese custom Nihon no shūkan

CUSTOM

'Proper behaviour' in Japan involves both verbal and non-verbal customs which take a lifetime to master. There is even an 'Ogasawara School of Etiquette', dating back hundreds of years, where young people (especially young ladies about to be married) can learn how to behave 'properly' in society. Compared to this, even the most polite Westerner looks and behaves like the proverbial bull in a china shop. But don't despair – the Japanese have long ago learned to make allowances for **hen na gaijin** (strange outside people) like you and me. However, since treading on Japanese toes does hurt them in the long run, it is worth knowing a few major customs so as to get off their toes occasionally. Besides, if you were able to act exactly like a well-bred Japanese, you would be just as strange! Thus, what is to be done? The ideal of the old-style English 'gentleman' comes to mind, who is friendly and reticent, ready to learn, and able to laugh at himself (but who doesn't laugh at the customs of the 'funny natives'). Japanese culture has been going strong for two thousand years, so Western 'cultural imperialism' is uncalled for. The Japanese have, on their own, taken over many Western customs, e.g. in dress (*see* CLOTHES) and food (*see* BREAKFAST), but rejected others (e.g. there is virtually no handshaking among Japanese).

Politeness is invariably shown to high-status guests, among whom you will be numbered, but this also means that the feeling of really becoming an intimately trusted insider is forever denied. A formal reserve or **enryo** characterizes Japanese interpersonal behaviour, in strong contrast to their Korean neighbours. No wonder that Eton- and Oxbridge-educated English nobility is still regarded as a model of proper behaviour – but should you start imitating them?

customer (*of company*) tokui-saki, o-kyaku-san
  you're a very important customer (anata wa) totemo
  taisetsu na tokui-saki des

Customs zeikan　税関

D

dark kurai

date tsuki-hi
  what's the date? nan-nichi des ka?
  let's fix a date kijitsu o kimemashō

DATES

Dates on documents are written in the international
style, i.e. year – month – day. For overseas correspondence the Christian method of counting years
(called **seireki**) is used – 1987, 1988 1989 etc.
However, for internal consumption the prevalent
method for counting years is a system based on the
current Emperor's year of reign (**nengō**). Japanese
post offices therefore cancel stamps with two kinds
of post marks, depending on whether the letter will
leave the country or not. For conversions between
1926 and 1988 (i.e. during the reign of Emperor
Hirohito, the so-called **Shōwa** era), 25 has to be
added to or subtracted from the last two digits of the
year as counted according to the Western system.
The year 1988 is equivalent to 63 in the Japanese
system, called **Shōwa** – the era of 'Enlightened
Peace'. Thus the Second World War in Japan ended
in **Shōwa** 20 (1945 minus 25).

As an example:

  18 April 1987

is called:

  **Shōwa roku-jū-ni-nen (no) shi-gatsu jū-hachi-
  nichi**

This means literally:

  Shōwa sixty-second year, fourth month, eighteenth day

You can also say:

  **Sen-kyū-hyaku-hachi-jū-nana-nen (no) shi-gatsu
  jū-hachi-nichi**

which means literally:

  thousand nine hundred eighty-seven years
  fourth month eighteenth day

  When the Emperor dies, the Crown Prince as-
cends the throne, a special committee convenes to
choose a new era name (or **nengō**) and that year

becomes Year 1 (**gan-nen**) of the new era. Thus, when Emperor Hirohito died on 7 January 1989, Crown Prince Akihito ascended the throne and the new **nengō Heisei** ('achievement of universal peace') was announced. 1989 was thus **Shōwa 64** for seven days before giving way to **Heisei 1** (**Heisei gan-nen**). From 1989 onwards, 88 has to be added or subtracted accordingly: 1990 is **Heisei ni-nen**, 1991 is **Heisei san-nen**, etc.

daughter musume

day hi

The days of the week in Japanese are:

Monday	getsu-yōbi	[moon day]
Tuesday	ka-yōbi	[fire day]
Wednesday	sui-yōbi	[water day]
Thursday	moku-yōbi	[wood day]
Friday	kin-yōbi	[gold day]
Saturday	do-yōbi	[earth day]
Sunday	nichi-yōbi	[sun day]

Some useful phrases are:

on Monday
getsu-yōbi ni

on what day?
nan-yōbi des ka?

At present the Western idea of weekends is becoming popular, though many schools and shops still function on Saturdays. As Japan is a non-Christian country, Sunday is the great day for going out and shopping. Avoid public transport into the countryside on this day! Shops, especially department stores, usually close on one of the weekdays, museums usually on Mondays. Increasingly, 24-hour shops for general provisions have become numerous. They never close, since they are staffed at night by university students doing **arubaito** (part-time work, from the German *Arbeit* = work).

dead: he is dead (kare wa) shinde imas

deal: it's a deal sore ni kimari des

December jū-ni-gatsu

declare: nothing to declare shinkoku suru mono wa arimasen

delay (*noun*) okure
  he's been delayed (kare wa) okurete imas

delicious oishī

A useful phrase to use after a meal is:

> **go-chisō-sama deshta**

which means literally:

> it was a feast

This is said to your host on leaving, with a slight bow. It can also be used towards the staff of a restaurant on leaving to show appreciation, especially since there is no tipping. At Japanese universities almost all Japanese students say it to the lady behind the counter doing the washing-up when they deposit their dirty dishes in front of her.

dentist ha-isha

dentures sō-ireba [so-ee-re-ba]

diarrhoea geri

diary nikki

dictionary jisho

DICTIONARY FORM

The 'dictionary form' is the first form given for translations of verbs (and sometimes adjectives). It is contrasted with the 'polite form', which is given afterwards between obliques and which ends in **-mas**. The latter is the form that you and your Japanese partners are most likely to use. *See also* PLAIN FORMS.

difference chigai

the main difference ichiban no chigai
it doesn't make any difference chigai ga arimasen

different chigau /chigaimas/

difficult: it's difficult muzukashī des

When used with verbs (e.g. 'difficult to see', 'difficult to read' etc.), the adjectival suffix **-nikui** is added to the 'verb stem' (*see* VERBS):

> **it's difficult to read these characters**
> kono kanji wa yominikui des

> **it's difficult to see (from here)**
> (koko kara) minikui des

> **the window was very difficult to open**
> mado wa hijō ni akinikukatta des

You will see from the last example that **akinikui** can have other forms, just as any adjective of this type can (*see* ADJECTIVES). It is also possible to put such adjectives before a noun:

> **yominikui kanji**
> 'difficult-to-read characters'

> **wakarinikui Nihongo**
> 'difficult-to-understand' Japanese

difficulty muzukashi-sa

DIMINUTIVES

These are not an important feature of Japanese. In the case of animals, the syllable **ko-** (which can mean both 'young' or 'small') precedes the word in question. For example:

cat	neko
kitten	ko-neko
dog	inu
puppy	ko-inu
horse	uma
foal, pony	ko-uma

Similarly, **ko-** or **shō-** (small) can be added to other nouns. For example:

bottle	bin
small bottle	ko-bin
town	toshi
small town	shō-toshi

The suffix **-chan**, added to someone's name, can also be seen as a diminutive, although it is probably derived from a childish mispronunciation of the suffix **-san**. Small children are usually addressed by an abbreviated form of their given name plus **-chan** until they reach the age of about ten (although the family and close friends can use it after this).

A Miss Kobayashi Michiko in her mid-twenties will thus be addressed in everyday life as:

> **Kobayashi-san**
> Miss Kobayashi

by female friends from her high school days or before as :

> **Michiko-san**
> Miss Michiko

by her very close friends, parents and older brothers and sisters as:

> **Michiko-chan**
> little Michiko

and when she was small, and sometimes still by her parents, especially if she is the youngest in the family, as:

Mit-chan
little Mi

dinner yūshoku

DINNER

Traditionally, Japanese breakfast, lunch and dinner were quite similar: rice in large helpings, with extras, such as fish, pickles etc., according to taste and affluence. Food should be served to look beautiful, and the colour combinations and shapes not only of the food, but also of their containers, should harmonize. Traditionally, beer (or other alcohol) was served only after the meal, since alcohol and rice don't go together in the eyes (or rather mouths) of the Japanese. However, this is not strictly observed any more. In families where the husband works far away from home (these days, the majority in Japan), dinner can often not be shared with the children, except at weekends. The wife thus has to keep dinner ready for whenever **danna-san** (the honourable master) makes his appearance, often near midnight. Only weekends allow many families to be complete round the table for dinner. It is of help here that traditional Japanese food can be eaten cold or lukewarm. Large electric containers keep food and drink, such as rice and green tea, warm for many hours. For futher comments, *see* BREAKFAST and FOOD.

direct chokusetsu
  direct flight chokkōbin

director kanri-yaku-in
  (*member of board of directors*) torishimariyaku

dirty yogoreta, kitanai

disadvantage furi

discount (*noun*) nebiki

discussion giron

dish (*plate*) sara
  (*meal*) ryōri

diskette disketto
  on diskette disketto de

distance kyori
what's the distance from . . . to . . .? . . . kara . . .
made dore kurai des ka?

distribution (*of goods*) bumpai-butsu

divorced: he's/I'm divorced rikon shte imas

do suru /shimas/
can you do that? sore ga dekimas ka?
what are you doing? nani o shte imas ka?

doctor (*medical*) isha 医者
(*polite form*) o-isha-san
(*academic*) hakase

DOCTORS

Traditionally, Japan has been strongly influenced by
German medicine. So much so that older doctors
still converse in German with each other in front of
their patients so as not to be understood. Medical
attention can range from mediocre to excellent,
especially at the big city hospitals. If you fall ill,
phone the English-speaking information service
(Tokyo 502-1461; from outside Tokyo: phone 104
and ask for 'Collect Call, T.I.C.'). They will give you
advice about the nearest English-speaking doctor.
There are also some Western doctors practising in
the large cities, and their names can likewise be
obtained from the above numbers. Furthermore,
there are some large hospitals, such as St Luke's or
the Seventh Day Adventist Hospital, where you can
get help from Western doctors.

Most Japanese belong to the national health
insurance scheme which pays 70 per cent of medical
costs. You may have to be resident in Japan for a
year before you can qualify.

document shorui

door doa [doh-a]

doorway genkan

double: double gin jin no dabburu
double room futari-beya

down: the price has come down genka wa sagarimashta
down there sono shta des

down payment atama-kin

downtown Tokyo Tōkyō no shtamachi

draft (*of agreement*) sōan

dress (*for woman*) doresu
   (*clothing*) ifuku
   See CLOTHES

drink (*noun*) nomimono
   (*alcoholic*) arukōru, o-sake
   would you like a drink? nomimono wa ikaga des ka?
   (*alcoholic*) o-sake wa ikaga des ka?
   thanks but I don't drink dōmo, demo o-sake wa
   nomimasen

DRINK

Alcohol is freely available in Japan – even in
vending machines, which dispense beer, whisky and
sake. Drinking time is after work, so lunch-time
drinking is unusual. However, once it gets dark,
drinking is regarded as an acceptable way to relax.

Anti-alcoholic company employees (or those with
a really weak stomach) have a hard time in Japan. Of
course you can stick to soft drinks when being
invited for a drink as long as you can act the part of
the inebriated group member! Women are also free
to drink, but they should not give any indication of
being drunk – a male 'prerogative' in Japan (*see*
DRUNKENNESS).

It can become very expensive if you go drinking
on your own. Some bars display no prices. Although
Japanese are reluctant to do so, you might ask what a
bottle of beer costs and then decide to stay or to
leave:

> **how much is a bottle of beer?**
> bīru ip-pon wa ikura des ka?

> **please write down the price**
> nedan o kaite kudasai

Beware of hostess bars, and places serving you
little titbits, such as rice crackers or peanuts – these
can push up the price sky-high.

The safest places to go for a drink are bars run by
the large liquor companies, Suntory or Nikka – you
will see their signs outside. They usually have
standard prices. Other inexpensive places are beer
halls, often situated on the top floor of department
stores.

The most popular choices:

Japanese males mostly drink whisky. Scots (and
not only they) will be surprised to find how many
good Japanese brands exist, and how many Scotch
labels there are which they never dreamed of.

Whisky is drunk with lots of water and ice – this combination is called **mizu-wari**.

Beer has become very popular, and the Japanese brands, mostly modelled on German lager beer, are very good indeed. Beer is always served chilled.

Sake (pronounced sah-ke) is the general term for alcoholic drinks, as well as the word for Japanese rice wine. The latter, containing about 17 per cent alcohol, can be roughly compared to sherry in its effects. It is a holy drink, and **sake** cups are exchanged between bride and groom during their wedding ceremony. Furthermore, **sake** is drunk to hail New Year's Day – a special kind of sweet **sake** flavoured with herbs and called **o-toso**. **Sake** is mostly served hot (except on the above occasions, or in summer) and is poured into very small containers (**sakazuki**) which are then emptied at a gulp.

The pouring of drinks should always be done reciprocally. Lift up your cup when somebody offers to fill it for you and observe the seniority rule: juniors pour for seniors, females for males, and hosts for guests. After that, the order can be reversed. All this calls for a lot of jolly attention – *see* TOASTS. *See also* ALCOHOL.

driving licence unten-menkyo-shō

drunk: he's drunk yopparatte imas

DRUNKENNESS

Drunkenness among males is condoned in Japan, as long as it occurs in the right places (e.g. bars) and at the right time (in the evening, after work). Since most men are under heavy pressure during the day, having to cope with complicated human relationships, evenings are the only time they can relax. In fact, at least once a year, during the year-end party, one can get drunk with one's boss and tell him exactly (well, almost . . .) what one thinks of him. In some groups, such occasions are more frequent. Such outpourings are said not to be held against their perpetrator.

Females may drink, but should not advertise the effects in public – while males often act drunk to be accepted as part of the group they are with (*see also* DRINK).

dry (*air, ground*) kansō shta
(*towels, throat*) kawaita

(*wine*) karakuchi (no)

dry-cleaner's dorai-kurīningu, kurīningnya-san

during . . . . . . no aida
    during the summer vacation natsu-yasumi no aida

dwarf trees bonsai

E

each: how much are they each? hitotsu wa ikura des ka?
    each of them sore-zore (no)

ear mimi

early (*arrive*) hayaku
    early in the morning asa hayaku

east higashi
    in the East tōhō (no)

Easter Īsutā

EASTER
Easter celebrations are unknown in Japan, which is very little affected by Christian customs.

easy yasashī

eat taberu /tabemas/
    something to eat nanika taberu mono

EATING HABITS
While Western food and table manners are known, they co-exist with native ones. Japanese food (based largely on rice, with many kinds of side dishes) is usually served all at once, and eaten with chopsticks. Everything except the rice and bean curd soup is likely to be cold, or at best tepid. The emphasis is on the preservation of the natural flavour and on beautiful appearance. The colours and shapes of the food should harmonize with the dishes.

On starting, everyone bows slightly and says **Itadakimas**. Literally translated, this means 'I receive' (from a superior), and is the equivalent of the French *bon appétit*.

Frequently hand towels (**o-shibori**), hot in winter and cold in summer, are distributed on sitting down at the table. You may already have come across this custom on your flight to Japan.

Disposable chopsticks, made from natural wood, are split apart for use. Slurping noises while drinking soup or eating noodles are quite acceptable, as is the picking of one's teeth after the meal.

Green tea, served at the end, is never taken with additives, such as sugar or milk. After the meal one says:

> **go-chisō-sama deshta!**
> it was a feast!

to the host, or to the restaurant staff on departure. *See also* BREAKFAST, DINNER, FOOD, FORMALITY, LUNCH, RESTAURANTS.

economy: the Japanese economy Nihon keizai

either: either one dochira-demo
either . . . or . . . . . . ka . . . ka

electric denki (no)

electronics denshin-gaku

else: something else sono-hoka-ni
somewhere else doko-ka hoka-no tokoro
someone else dare-ka hoka-no hito

embarrassing hazukashī

EMBARRASSMENT

In Japan, where formality and proper etiquette are very important, embarrassing situations can happen to you frequently, since you cannot be expected to know all the detailed rules of conduct. Be prepared to apologize frequently, e.g. by saying '**sumimasen**', etc. (*see* SORRY). A few examples of embarrassing situations are:

> not taking off your shoes on entering a private home or a Japanese-style restaurant;
> not taking off your slippers when walking on **tatami** mats in a house;
> coming too close to your Japanese partner when conversing;
> kissing or embracing in public;
> eating in the streets;
> talking too informally and/or too loudly;
> praising yourself or members of your own group (this can include your employer and your compatriots);
> keeping too much eye contact.

It is hard to know at first whether you have caused embarrassment, since Japanese, keen on preserving harmony, are good at covering up, for example by smiling to hide their embarrassment. Furthermore, they are mostly too polite and too worried about your possible loss of face to correct you. Advice from a knowledgeable outsider may sometimes be invaluable when your behaviour seems to have given offence. Above all, try never to get angry or to lose your temper! *See also* CUSTOMS, GUESTS.

embassy: the British embassy Igirisu (Eikoku) taishkan

Emperor of Japan Tennō Heika

empty (*adjective*) kara (no)

end (*noun: of period of time, of road*) owari
end of the month getsumatsu

England Igirisu *or* Eikoku イングランド
Both these words usually imply the whole of the United Kingdom. If you want to refer to England specifically you can use: **Ingurando**. *See* BRITAIN

English (*adjective*) Igirisu (Eikoku) no
(*language*) Eigo (no)
I'm English Igirisu-jin des
I'm British Eikokujin des
do you speak English? Eigo o hanashimas ka?

ENGLISH

Although English is virtually the only foreign language taught widely in Japan, and although more than 90 per cent have struggled with it at school for six years, lamentably few are able to speak it fluently and with confidence. The major reason is that the infamous entrance exams to the next higher step in one's education require knowledge of written English only. English is thus taught rather like Latin in the West – as a dead language, whose intricacies must be memorized and regurgitated on demand during examinations. Those who want to learn spoken, everyday English must turn to one of the many private language schools.

Although much is written every year lamenting this situation, improvement is unlikely for various reasons, of which the most important ones are:

(a) The vested interest which the many Japanese teachers of English have in the status quo. Brought up in the very same system, most are unable to conduct a fluent conversation with a native English speaker, but are well versed in the explanation of intricate English forms of grammar or literature (by using Japanese).

(b) The peculiarities of the Japanese language. Several important sounds vital for pronouncing English correctly are missing: there is no distinctive 'l' sound (for which 'r' is substituted in foreign loan words); there is no 'v' (thus substituted by 'b'), and in Japanese every consonant must be followed by a vowel, except for the letter 'n'. When attempting to speak English, this often leads to a mixture one could call either 'Japlish' or 'Janglish', turning 'I loved her in Venice' into 'Ai rubbed hāru in Benisu'. Since most Japanese first come across a Western word when written in **katakana** (*see* WRITING SYSTEM), it is easy to see why even college professors might address their letter to someone in **Rondon** (London), since in their mind's eye it is in the **katakana** form of 'ro-n-do-n' – there being no way to distinguish between 'lo' and 'ro' in written Japanese.

(c) Social etiquette demands that one does not contradict one's superiors (*see* POLITENESS LEVELS). Japanese have very little chance to interact with native English speakers who might correct them at an early age. They thus acquire bad habits of pronunciation which nobody dares to correct once they are older, as this may lead to loss of face. Since second-language learning frequently involves the making of stupid mistakes and being laughed at (which Westerners can stomach more easily), Japanese are strongly disadvantaged in this respect. That motivated Japanese can learn to speak English fluently is shown by institutions which stress language learning as verbal communication, e.g. the International Christian University in Tokyo, where every Japanese first-year student has to take an intensive course in English for one whole year before starting lectures. This method can produce amazing results, with the use of native speakers and properly supervised language lab training.

(d) Related to (c) is the experience of the few Japanese fluent in English of being looked down upon by other Japanese as somehow 'eccentric' or even 'unpatriotic'. This goes so far that some try to hide this ability when in the company of their compatriots. Furthermore, those good at English are often shunted into interpreters' jobs on joining a company and thus have no hope of getting into the decision-making group.

In spite of all this, Westerners should not gloat – how many are able to conduct a conversation with Japanese tourists or businessmen in Japanese?

enough jūbun (na)
  not enough jūbun de nai
  that's enough, thank you jūbun des, dōmo!

entrance iriguchi 入口
  (*to house*) genkan

envelope fūtō

essential: that's essential sore wa fukaketsu des
  no, that's not essential sore wa fukaketsu ja arimasen

estimate (*noun*) mitsumori
  it's only an estimate (sore wa) mitsumori dake des

Europe Yōroppa
  in Europe Yōroppa dewa

evening ban
  this evening komban
  good evening komban wa!

every subete no

everyone minna
  hello everyone min-na-san kon-nichi wa!

everything subete
  well, I think that's everything (*said at end of meeting etc.*) dewa, ijō des

excellent steki (na)
  excellent! steki des!

exchange rate kawase sōba
  what is the exchange rate for the pound? pondo no kawase sōba wa dore kurai des ka?

excuse me (*to get attention*) sumimasen
  (*apology*) sumimasen
  excuse me, could you tell me where . . .? sumimasen, . . . wa doko des ka?

exhausted: I'm exhausted totemo tsukarete imas

exhibition (*trade fair etc.*) tenrankai

exit deguchi 出口

expenses: it's on expenses hitsuyō-keihi ni fukumarete imas

expensive takai

expiry date (*of visa etc.*) saigo no hi [*literally: the last day*]

explain: could you explain that to me? sore o setsumei shte kudasaimas ka?

export (*verb*) yushutsu suru /shimas/
we export . . . . . . o yushutsu shimas
our export campaign (watakshi-tachi no) yushutsu undō

export director yushutsu sekinin-sha

express: by express mail sokutatsu de

express train tokkyū

expression (*on face*) hyōjō
See FACIAL EXPRESSIONS

extension: extension 334 (*telephone*) naisen no san-san-yon
(*of contract*) kei-yaku enchō

extra: there are no extra charges tsuika-ryōkin wa arimasen
is that extra? sore wa tsuika-bun des ka?

eye me

eye contact me-sen

EYE CONTACT

In formal situations Japanese make far less eye contact than Westerners. It is considered polite not to look superiors in the eye, but ideally to fix one's gaze slightly lower, for example on the tie knot. As opposed to Western greetings, where one shakes hands and looks one's partner in the eye, Japanese bowing requires no body contact and the casting-down of one's eyes. This is easily interpreted as shiftiness, especially by Americans, and can hinder the building-up of reciprocal trust. Japanese, too, after long residence in the United States, mention that they are regarded as being 'too forthright' because of their tendency to make more eye contact. If you have a chance to look at Japanese television or films, take a note of the way two persons speak to each other – their eye contact is much reduced and often altogether absent when they converse.

F

face kao

FACE – LOSS OF

In a culture where opinions of other persons (especially those of one's seniors) are very important, the concept of **kao** ('face') is used in many expressions, for example:

> **to save face**
> kao o tateru [*literally: to set up face*]

> **to lose face**
> kao o tsubureru [*literally: to smash face*]

> **to cause someone else to lose face**
> kao o tsubusu

> **to be influential**
> kao ga kiku [*literally: the face has effect*]

> **to be widely recognized**
> kao ga hiroi [*literally: the face is wide*]

> **a person of influence**
> kao-yaku [*literally: face service*]

> **to extend one's influence**
> kao o uru [*literally: to sell one's face*]

To avoid losing face is of the utmost importance. This can be achieved either defensively or in an aggressive way, and explains much about Japanese behaviour. Some defensive ways are the following:

Avoid direct self-exposure which risks causing shame. Control your expression, and suppress your natural feelings or sympathies, while acting in a predetermined, ritualistic way. Such reserve keeps others at bay. This distance is expressed both emotionally (e.g. by very polite behaviour) and physically (e.g. by bowing).

In the extreme case do and SAY nothing at all, and present a poker face to the world. This happens if a well-rehearsed behaviour pattern is not known or unavailable. On meeting a stranger (e.g. a Westerner) who could be important, a 'freezing' often occurs to save face, since you do not know what is expected. Such behaviour is often experienced by Westerners, who therefore tend to believe that it occurs more commonly in Japan than is really the case.

Defending your face also means defending that of your opposite number – thus it is vitally important not to embarrass others. The interaction then becomes ritualized since both of you are keen to preserve discretion. Many polite phrases are exchanged which do not really show much individualistic thought and feeling.

What is done in a practical way to avoid losing face? Frequently, go-betweens are employed to take the blame should anything go wrong. This is especially so in arranged marriages between two families.

Furthermore, one often refuses to state something outright, but expects one's partner to guess it. The burden is then on the receiver of such a message. The vagueness and understatement of the Japanese language help one to retract more easily if something goes wrong. For example, the reply to an offer, **kekkō des** [*literally: it is fine*], means both 'I appreciate it' as well as 'no thank you'.

Japanese therefore often feel very tense when having to use English because it commits them to direct action much more easily, and forces them to make assertive statements which cannot easily be retracted.

When one behaves unobtrusively and (seemingly) modestly, face can be defended. Shyness and humility can even be used as a weapon, forcing one's opposite to start insisting on something, and thus becoming vulnerable.

To reduce uncertainties, much interaction is ritualized. One-upmanship at gatherings is disliked. At meetings and parties there is a well-rehearsed taking of turns when speaking up. To avoid losing face can also make aggressive behaviour necessary. However, since this is officially frowned upon in Japanese society, it has to be done very discreetly. Generosity shown to others can be quite aggressive, e.g. entertaining lavishly, and insisting on paying the bill. Stinginess is greatly despised. If there is a clear rank in a group, the most senior person is expected to pay. Moreover, on paying, one must seem to be indifferent to money, e.g. at a bar which is far more expensive than was expected. This situation of course occurs rarely, since one goes there initially with somebody whom one knows and can trust. Change should not be counted, even if one seems to have been cheated. It is bad form to query the bill and to make a fuss.

face mask (*for colds*) masku

FACIAL EXPRESSIONS

One Japanese word for 'face' (**men**) is the same word as for 'mask'. As opposed to the 'let it all hang out' attitude of many Westerners, Japanese do not like to show their emotions, especially in formal situations. From childhood onwards they are taught to control their facial muscles more than most Westerners and to present a poker face to the outside world, or a pleasant smile which does not necessarily mean that they are brimming over with joy. This is in line with Japanese etiquette – to present as pleasant an exterior as possible, even though the subject of conversation may not be exactly mirthful. Westerners are disconcerted by a smiling Japanese who tells them that their father has just died – in the West we expect more congruence between topic and outward behaviour, while in Japan it is imperative that one appear as pleasant as possible to a high-status guest even if the news is sad.

However, at drinking parties this reserve can change abruptly, and you might suddenly see some real emotions and be told some truths you had never bargained for. In all such situations, the stereotyped English gentleman's reserve will be an ideal worth emulating, though even then your Western facial expression can be read like an open book by most Japanese.

factory kōjō

fair (*commercial*) himpyō-kai

fall (*person*) ochiru /ochimas/
sales are falling uri-age ga ochite imas

family (*plain*) kazoku
(*polite*) go-kazoku
my family (watakshi no) kazoku
The 'plain' form is used for families in general or for one's own family.

FAMILY

Traditionally, the unit of Japanese society was the extended family, consisting of grandparents, their oldest son (as head of the house) with his wife, and the grandchildren. A better name for this kind of family would probably be 'house'. Unlike in China, whose Confucian system is also based on the close-knit extended family, Japanese custom allowed for the adoption of non-related persons into the family. For instance, if there was no son, or if the only son was no good, a future son-in-law from outside might be persuaded to give up his family name and connections and take on the family name of his wife, to become the head of her 'house'. In extreme cases, e.g. in the absence of children, a young girl might even be adopted into the 'house', be raised in its ways for many years, and then marry somebody who takes over the family name and responsibility for its continuation.

Although this system was discontinued after the Second World War, strong traces are still to be found. It also influenced many other organizations, e.g. business companies, in Japan, who even today tend to think in terms of the 'family' or 'house' as their ideal.

Since outside persons can be introduced into the system and made full members through a long apprenticeship, the feeling of continuity is very strong in many Japanese companies. While the image of the 'happy family' is often loudly pro-claimed (e.g. in company songs, after-hours socializing, etc.), the reality might be different. However, group cohesion is usually so strong that Japanese do not broadcast their intra-group quarrels to the outside world.

From this it follows that Western (especially American) companies operating in Japan will attract quite a different kind of Japanese employee – usually one who objects to this (often enforced) closeness, and who is more independent-minded.

family Buddhist altar butsudan

fan (*hand-held*) ōgi

far tōi
    how far is it to . . .? . . . made dore kurai tōi des ka?
    is it far? tōi des ka?

Far East kyoku-tō

fast hayai
    it's too fast haya-sugimas

father (*own father*) chichi
  (*someone else's*) otō-san

faulty (*equipment*) ketten no aru

fax (*noun*) fakksu

February ni-gatsu

feel: how are you feeling? ikaga des ka?
  I'm feeling better mae yori ī des
  I feel like a . . . (*drink etc.*) . . . ga hoshī des

FEMININE FORMS

When Japanese came to be first written down by the earliest visitors from China over 1,600 years ago, it already contained elaborate courtesy levels. There were special words and phrases for praising one's superiors, and deprecating oneself or members of one's group. Since men were regarded as superior to women, especially in Confucian thinking, which has dominated Japan for the last 300 years, women's speech was invariably more polite (*see also* POLITE-NESS LEVELS).

In pre-war Japan the differences between male and female speech patterns were much more pronounced than they are today, but there are still many forms and words exclusively used by either men or women. This poses a problem for those Western men who have learned the language from their Japanese wives or girlfriends only. In such cases the latter are sometimes called **ne-jibiki** (sleeping dictionaries) behind their back . . . When such men start to speak Japanese in polite society, the results can be quite hilarious. It is rather as if, say, a German had learned all his English in rural India and was under the mistaken impression that this was the regular way to speak it at the Queen's garden party.

Some clear-cut distinctions between males and females are the following:

1. Males speak with a more even tone of voice, which can sound rather like staccato machine-gun fire when spoken fast and in anger, while females inflect their voices more, so that their Japanese sounds a little more 'lilting'. English makes far more use of inflections (e.g. 'I want *this* one!' versus '*I* want this one!'), while in Japanese such differences are conveyed by changing the particles after 'I' and 'this'. Likewise, for questions the voice does not have to be raised at the end of the sentence, since the question marker **-ka** indicates this condition.

Therefore, native English speakers will already have a 'feminine' inflexion when they speak Japanese, since this is a basic habit acquired from one's mother tongue which is almost impossible to unlearn. Of course, such a 'roller coaster' way of speaking is something which Japanese have come to expect from Westerners.

In the realm of public speaking there is very little difference between the sexes concerning intonation, words and phrases used. Needless to say, both use very polite, formal speech. The picture changes once we get to personal conversations. In an all-male company of friends, the tone can be very short, rough and typically 'masculine'. Once women enter this sphere, the language used will contain many more polite forms, something women tend to use in each other's company as well, even among friends. It can therefore be said that modern developments in city life, where many more women have entered business since the war, have caused everyday speech to become more polite and, in this way, more 'feminine'.

2. Differences in pronouns – *see* 1.

3. Differences in interjections. Apart from many other different interjections, men in informal speech tend to use **-zo** or **-ze** at the end of sentences to emphasize what they want to say, while females will use **-wa**, for example:

> **this sake is really good!**

would be conveyed as follows by a Japanese male:

> kono sake umai-ze!
> [*this sake delicious is (emphatic)*]

and by a Japanese female:

> kono o-sake wa oishī-wa!
> [*this (honorific) sake (subject) delicious is (emphatic)*]

4. Women will make more use of the polite prefix **o-** or **go-**, as in:

> **o-denwa** (*feminine*) versus **denwa** (*masculine*)
> (your) telephone

> **o-sake** (*especially used by bar hostesses*) versus **sake** (*masculine*)
> (your) sake

> **o-toire** (*feminine*) versus **toire** (*masculine*)
> (your) toilet

Women also tend to use some emotional interjections more than men, such as 'cute!' (**kawaī**) or 'marvellous!' (**steki!**). To express surprise when meeting somebody unexpectedly, females will tend to say:

mā! or **ara!**

which are never used by men, who will tend to say:

yā! or **ō!**

One consequence of this is that, in novels featuring informal conversations between a man and a woman, a Japanese author need not tell the reader who is who – all is clear from their way of speaking, especially from the sentence endings.

5. Japanese does not have feminine forms in the European-language sense of 'manager/manageress'.

ferry ferī

few: just a few hon no skoshi
  a few days ni-san-nichi
  a few minutes ni-san-pun
  a few drinks ni-san-bai

figure (*number*) sūji
  can we see the figures? sūji o mite mo ī des ka?
  See COUNTING OBJECTS

filling (*in tooth*) tsume-mono

film (*for camera*) firumu
  (*at cinema*) eiga

final saigo (no)
  that's our final offer (sore wa) saigo no tei-an des

finance director zai-sei sekinin-sha

find mitskeru /mitskemas/

fine: that's fine (sore wa) des

finger yubi

finish owaru /owarimas/
  I haven't finished (*meal etc.*) mada des

fire (*for heating*) hi
  (*destructive*) kaji

first (*adjective*) saisho (no)
  at first hajime ni
  this is my first time in Japan Nihon wa hajimete des

first class (*travel etc.*) (*on aeroplanes*) fāsto kuras
  (*on Japanese Railways, 'Green Car'*) gurīn-sha

first name namae

FIRST NAMES

Japanese invariably have only one first name (more correctly called 'given name'), which is traditionally placed after the family name, and is never abbreviated in addresses or on name cards. It should not be used on its own for addressing anyone – although in the case of children the given name can be used, if followed by **-chan** (up to the age of ten or so) and **-san**, if older. In case of doubt, use the family name and **-san**. Unlike Westerners, Japanese use the given name only rarely – even inside the family it is only the more senior person who calls the junior one in this way, while in reply the senior person's title is used. For example:

o-nē-san (*formal*)

or:

o-nē-chan (*intimate*)

for:

older sister

-o-kā-san (*formal*)

or:

o-kā-chan (*intimate*)

for:

mother

Even childhood friends call one another rarely by given name only: usually **-san** or **-chan** is added, and once past the age of about fifteen, new friends are called by family name and **-san**. Therefore, avoid the American urge to call Japanese by first name only. If expressly invited to do so, for example by those Japanese who have lived abroad for a long time, it is always safer to use given name with the polite suffix **-san**. For example:

Mr SHIMAZU Akira

can then be called:

Akira-san

If this privilege has been granted to you in a very informal setting, while getting drunk with him for instance, you might revert to:

Shimazu-san

when sober and in the company of his colleagues.

Since Westerners have their name cards printed in the order where given (Christian) name precedes the family name, many Japanese might address you by given name and **-san**, thinking that this is your family name.

See also ADDRESSING PEOPLE, BUSINESS CARDS, CHRISTIAN NAMES, LETTERS, NAME, SURNAMES

fish (*noun*) sakana

flat (*apartment*) apāto

flight kōkū-bin
my flight is at ... bin wa ... des

flight number kōkū-bin no bangō

floor yuka
on the ground floor ikkai ni

FLOORS

The Japanese count floors as in America – the British ground floor is the Japanese first floor, the British first floor is the Japanese second floor etc.: ground floor **ikkai**, first floor **nikai**, followed by **sangai, yonkai, gokai, rokkai** etc.

flower hana
a bunch of flowers ichiwa no hana

flower arranging ikebana

flu ryūkan

fly (*verb*) tobu /tobimas/

food tabemono　食べ物

FOOD

A traditional Japanese meal is made up of staple foods, plus side dishes. The word for meal, '**gohan**', also means 'rice', attesting to its fundamental importance (*see* EATING HABITS). As more and more Japanese also eat Western foods, especially when they go to a restaurant, many new words, mainly from English, have been Japanized to describe previously unfamiliar items. The most important ones are included in the list below:

STAPLE FOODS
boiled rice　　　　　　　　gohan *or* meshi
barley　　　　　　　　　　ōmugi
noodles　　　　　　　　　udon, soba

RICE DISHES
rice, fried　　　　　　　　chāhan

rice steamed in fish bouillon with pieces of meat, fish and vegetable	kamameshi
rice balls wrapped in seaweed	nigiri
small rice balls with raw fish	sushi
mixed sushi on rice	chirashi-zushi
mixed sushi	gomoku-zushi
Osaka-style sushi cut in squares	oshi-zushi
rice in a bowl, with something on top	domburi
– with pork and vegetables	chūka domburi
– with broiled eel	unagi domburi
– with chicken and egg	oyako domburi
– with onions cooked in egg	tamago domburi
– with deep-fried shrimps	tendon
– with sliced beef	nikudon
– with deep-fried breaded pork cutlets in eggs	katsudon
rice, seasoned, wrapped in fried bean curd	inari-zushi
rice, sliced roll, vegetables and fish powder wrapped in seaweed	nori-maki
rice, seasoned, wrapped in seaweed, with cucumber	kappa-maki
fried rice with chicken	chikin raisu
steamed rice in fish bouillon with chicken	tori gohan

NOODLE DISHES

buckwheat noodles, long brownish	soba
Chinese noodles	rāmen
Chinese noodles in pork bouillon	chāshūmen
Chinese noodles in pork bouillon with bean paste	miso-rāmen
Chinese noodles in salted pork-flavoured soup with vegetables	kantom-men
Chinese noodles in salted bouillon with vegetables	champon
noodle-like squares containing minced pork and leeks, served in soup with noodles	wantam-men
wheatflour noodles, long, thick, white	udon
wheatflour noodles, long, thin, white	sōmen
noodles served cold, to be dipped into sweetened soy sauce	mori soba
noodles fried on griddle with	

small pieces of vegetable	yaki soba
noodles in pork broth with bean sprouts	moyashi soba
noodles in fish broth	kake soba
noodles in fish bouillon with deep-fried shrimps	tempura soba
noodles in fish bouillon with boiled or raw egg on top	tsukimi soba
noodles in fish broth with rice cake	chikara udon
noodles in fish broth with bean curd	kitsune udon
noodles in fish bouillon with pork or beef	niku namban
noodles in broth with pieces of vegetable and meat	gomok soba

VEGETABLES

asparagus	asparagas
bamboo shoots	take-no-ko
bean curd	tōfu
bean curd (fried)	abura-age
beans	mame
cabbage	k'yabets
carrot	ninjin
corn on the cob, roasted	tōmorokoshi
croquettes	korokke
cucumber	k'yūri
eggplant	nasu
ginger	shōga
green pepper	pīman
lettuce	retass
mushroom	matsutake
mushroom (Japanese style)	shītake
onion	tamanegi
pickled vegetables	tsukemono
potatoes	jaga-imo
seaweed	nori
soy sauce	shōyu
soybeans	daizu
soybeans (fermented)	nattō
soybeans (fermented paste)	miso
spinach	hōrensō
tomato	tomato
yam, baked	yaki-imo

SEAFOOD

abalone	awabi
bass	suzuki
blowfish	fugu
bonito	katsuo

carp	koi
clams	hamaguri
cod	tara
cod roe	tarako
conger eel	anago
crab	kani
eel	unagi
eel (broiled, on rice)	unajū
eel (grilled, on rice)	unadon
fish, charcoal-grilled, with vegetables	robata-yaki
herring	nishin
herring roe	kazunoko
horse mackerel	aji
jellyfish, sliced, parboiled	kurage no sunomono
lobster	ise-ebi
mackerel	saba
octopus	tako
oyster	kaki
prawns	kuruma-ebi
raw fish	sashimi
raw fish on small rice balls	sushi, nigiri-zushi
salmon	sake
salmon (smoked)	smōk sāmon
salmon roe	ikura
sardines	iwashi
scallops	hotategai
sea bream	tai
sea urchin	uni
seafood, deep fried, with vegetables	tempura
shrimps	ebi
squid	ika
squid, charcoal-grilled	ika-yaki
sweet smelt	ayu
trout	masu
tuna	maguro
whale	kujira
yellowtail	buri

MEAT

beef	g'yū-niku
beef, cooked in soy sauce with ginger	g'yūniku no shōga-yaki
beef, sliced, with vegetables, cooked at the table	ski-yaki
beef, sliced, with vegetables, boiled at the table	shabu-shabu

beef and vegetables grilled at the table	teppan-yaki
beef steak	bifuteki
chicken	niwa-tori
chicken (roast)	rōsto chikin
chicken (grilled)	yaki-tori
chops	abara-niku
duck	ahiru
fillet	hire-niku
fowl	tori-niku
ham	hamu
hamburger	hambāga
liver	rebā
meat, grilled on skewers	kushi-yaki
meat-filled dumplings	niku-dango
on the bone	hone ts'ki
pork	buta-niku
pork, cooked in soy sauce with ginger	butashōga-yaki
pork, deep-fried, on rice	katsudon
pork, fried, marinated in soy sauce	yaki-niku
pork cutlets (deep fried)	tonkatsu
pork, minced, stuffed into fried dumplings	g'yōza
pork, sweet and sour	subuta
pork, small steamed balls in thin Chinese pastry	shūmai
quail	uzura
roast beef	rōsto-bīfu
roast pork	rōsto-pōku
sausage	sōsēji
sirloin	sāroin
spare ribs	speya-rib
sparrow	suzume
steak	stēki

SEASONING

fermented bean paste	miso
soy sauce	shōyu
sweetened rice wine	mirin

GENERAL INGREDIENTS

butter	batā
oil	abura
sugar	satō

SPICES

Cayenne pepper	tōgarashi

horseradish (Japanese)	wasabi
Japanese green onion	negi
mustard	karashi
pepper (Japanese)	sanshō
salt	shio
vinegar	su

SOUPS

fish and vegetable boiled in fish broth	oden
minestrone	minestorōne
noodle soups see noodle dishes (above)	
rice soups see rice dishes (above)	
soup with bean paste	miso-shiru
stock	dashi
tomato soup	tomato sūp

EGG DISHES

egg and fish custard	chawan-mushi
egg, steamed, on bean curd	tamago-dōfu
eggs, fried	medama-yaki
ham and eggs	hamu-eggu
omelette	omurets
omelette, Japanese style	tamago-yaki
omelette with rice	omurais

HORS D'OEUVRES

Japanese-style	o-tsumami
appetizer	tsukidashi

FRUIT

apples	ringo
bananas	banana
cherries	sakurambō
chestnuts	kuri
chestnuts, roasted	amaguri
coconuts	kōkonats
grapefruit	guēp-furūts
grapes	budō
lemons	remon
melons	meron
oranges	orenji
peaches	momo
pears (Japanese)	nashi
pears (Western)	yō-nashi
persimmons	kaki
pineapples	painappuru
plums (Japanese)	ume

plums (Western)	puramu
raspberries	ki-ichigo
strawberries	ichigo
tangerines	mikan
walnuts	kurumi
watermelons	suika

JAPANESE DRINKS

barley water	mugi-cha
distilled rice spirit	shōchū
rice wine	sake *or* Nihonshu
tea	o-cha

WESTERN FOODS AND DRINKS

beer	bīru
beer (draught)	nama-bīru
bread	pan
cheese roll	chīzu rōru
cocoa	kokoa
coffee	kōhī
cola	kōrā
curried rice	karei rais
ham sandwich	hamu sando
jam	jamu
marmalade	māmarēdo
milk	miruku *or* g'yū-n'yū
milk shake	miruku shēki
mineral water	mineraru uōtā
orange juice	orenji jūs
orange squash	orenji skash
pineapple juice	pa-in jūs
pork cutlets	tonkatsu
sandwiches	sandoichi
soda pop	saidā
spaghetti	spageti
tea (black)	kōcha
tea (black, with milk)	miruku tī
tea (black, with lemon)	remon tī
toast	tōsto
tomato juice	tomato jūs
tonic water	tonik uōtā
wine	budōshu
whisky	uiskī
whisky on the rocks	on-za-rokks
whisky with water	mizuwari

SWEETS, SNACKS

apple pie	appuru pai
bean paste, sweet, soft	yōkan
cake	kēki
candy floss	watagashi
cheese cake	chīzu-kēki
chocolate	chokorēto
cream puff	shūkurīm
crepe	kurēp
dessert	dezāto
doughnuts	dōnats
gelatin cubes and sweet beans with pieces of fruit	mitsumame
ice, crushed, with green tea soup	uji gōri
ice, crushed, with melon syrup	kōri meron
ice cream	aiskurīm
ice cream, on gelatin cubes, with sweet beans	kurīm
and fruit	am-mits
jelly	zerī
pancake, seasoned	okonomi-yaki
pineapple yoghurt	pa-in yōguruto
rice cakes	omochi
rice crackers	osembei
rice flour cakes with bean jam	manjū
sherbet	shābetto
shortcake	shōto kēki
soufflé	sufure
sponge cake	kastera
strawberry ice cream	storoberī aiskurīm
sweet bean soup with rice cake	oshiruko
vanilla egg custard with brown sugar	purin
vanilla ice cream	banira aiskurīm
yoghurt	yōguruto

To monolingual native English speakers the most puzzling Japanese name for a Western dish is probably **shūkurīm** for cream puffs (*see* the section on SWEETS). Do the Japanese really use shoe cream for their manufacture? The riddle is solved if one remembers that not all **gairai-go** (*see* LOAN WORDS) are derived from English. **Shūkurīmu** hails from French, where it is called *chou à la crème*!

American fast-food customs have also influenced Japanese cuisine. Apart from the ubiquitous Colonel

Sanders statues, advertising Kentucky Fried Chicken, and the **Makudonarudo** stores selling **hambāga**, one can now find Japanese lunch box shops, called **hoka hoka bentō**, just as one finds fish and chips shops in Britain.

foot (*on body*) **ashi**

Note that **ashi** is rather more vague than the English 'foot' since **ashi** can refer also to the leg:

ashi ga itai
my foot hurts/my leg hurts

for: for three nights (*e.g. room*) **san-paku**
this is for you anata ni des
that's for me watakshi ni des
are you for the idea? kono kangae ni sansei des ka?

foreign gaikoku (no)

foreign exchange (*money*) gaikoku kawase

foreigner gaikoku-jin

forget wasureru /wasuremas/
I forget wasuremashta
I didn't forget wasuremasen deshta
I forgot my briefcase here kaban o koko ni wasuremashta

fork (*for eating*) fōku

FORKS

Traditional Japanese cuisine does not call for any forks. Everything is cut up beforehand into such tiny bits that these can be lifted to one's mouth by the judicious use of chopsticks. Alternatively, food is presented in such a soft state that it can easily be separated by the use of the latter.

Japanese sometimes feel ill at ease during elaborate Western dinners, where they have to engage in the barbaric chopping and piercing of large chunks of meat on their dinner plates, confronted by a bewildering array of surgical knives and forks.

formal (*dinner, occasion*) seishiki (no)

FORMALITY

Japanese love of formality can be easily caricatured by Westerners, who are increasingly becoming less formal. The unsurpassed novel in this regard is

Thomas Raucat's *Honourable Picnic*, written in the twenties and re-published recently.

Knowledge about proper attire, gifts, things to say, things not to say etc., is drilled into most Japanese (especially females) from an early age. Complaints that university students 'don't have proper manners any more' cause more and more large companies to intensify the initial training for their new employees. Female recruits to a bank will for instance undergo elaborate training in the pouring of green tea for the bank's visitors, or in the 'correct' and beautiful-looking way of counting bank notes onto a tray before handing them over to the customer.

In many ways, Japan may remind one of descriptions of Victorian England, where proper ceremonial behaviour was essential on many occasions. This also means that the Westerner has to dress conservatively, and should know basic rules of Japanese etiquette.

The humid summers make wearing of jackets and ties a chore, but most Japanese will probably just comment, '**shikata ga nai**' ('it can't be helped'), and install even more air-conditioning.

When in doubt about what to do and to wear, try to get the advice of a Japanese friend or colleague beforehand.

free (*no cost*) tada

freight (*noun*) kamotsu

Friday kin-yōbi

fridge reizōko

fried rice yakimeshi

friend tomodachi

FRIENDS

In a culture where hierarchical relationships are so very important, and where people feel most secure when in contact with a person either superior or inferior to themselves in some way, true friendship based on equality is a rare thing. Japanese often remark that their true friends were made at kindergarten or primary school. After that, consciousness of rank intrudes, as is also shown by the fact that few non-related Japanese call one another by their given name after secondary school. It should therefore come as no surprise to hear of grandmothers going off to their kindergarten reunion!

from ...... kara
    from here to ... koko kara ... e
    from next month raigets kara
    this is a present from us tsumaranai mono deskedo, dōzo
    [*literally: it is a trifling thing, but please ...*]

front: in front of my hotel hoteru no mae de

FRONT

Beware of the loan word **furonto**, which means 'front desk'. Thus to meet at **hoteru no furonto** does *not* mean in front of the hotel, but at the front desk inside the hotel.

fruit kudamono

FRUIT

Because of the Yen's buying power, as well as modern refrigeration techniques, all the world's fruit can be bought in Japan these days – at a price. Department stores will wrap them carefully – *see* GIFTS.

However, many Westerners complain that relatively little fresh fruit is served during traditional-style dinners. The way in which it is cut and presented, however, can be a small miracle of beauty – *see* EATING HABITS.

Locally grown fruit is abundant, owing to the fact that the Japanese islands range from cool, apple-growing Hokkaido in the north to semi-tropical Okinawa in the south. Furthermore, plenty of winter sunshine allows fruit to be grown in plastic-covered hothouses, so that one can experience two crops of strawberries – one in January and one in summer. While the many kinds of apples, pears, cherries, plums and grapes are fairly similar to fruit available in Britain, there are also locally grown watermelons and oranges. One particular type of the latter is called **mikan** – the mandarin orange, usually first experienced by foreign visitors on long-distance trains when sold in fishnet containers holding about five or six. The golden persimmon (**kaki**) grows in many back yards all over the country. The persimmon has a diameter of about 2–3 inches, resembles a tomato and is yellow to red in colour. Unless very ripe it has an astringent taste.

One pleasant discovery is the **nashi**, with green or brown skin, while white inside, with hard, crunchy and exceptionally juicy flesh, tasting somewhat like a Western pear, but looking remarkably like a large apple. To distinguish them from Western-style pears, the latter are called **yō-nashi**, the **yō** being a general prefix for many things from the West.

For a list of fruit, and their names in Japanese, *see* FOOD.

full (*hotel etc.*) man-in
  no thanks, I'm full mō ī des, dōmo
  You could also say:

> **dōmo, mō kekkō des**
> thanks, I've had enough

Note also that in Japanese it is not impolite to refer directly to some bodily functions, such as:

> **my stomach is full**
> onaka ga ippai des

or:

> **my stomach is empty**
> onaka ga suite imas

fun: it's fun omoshiroi des

funny (*strange*) hen (na)
  (*comical*) omoshiroi

furniture kagu

FURNITURE

Western-style rooms in Japanese houses are generally smaller than equivalent rooms in the West. This means that the furniture, though in essence not much different, is generally smaller and more flimsy. This is especially so when Western-style furniture is placed in traditional Japanese rooms covered with **tatami** mats, since the latter are not meant to contain much furniture. Coupled with the general lack of storage space in urban homes, modern affluence gives most Japanese rooms a cluttered look.

Traditional Japanese living makes do with few items, and uncluttered space is regarded as the ideal. Even today, most newly built Japanese houses will contain at least one room laid out with **tatami** mats, on which one can sleep after spreading the quilted mattress (**futon**) at night and storing it in the deep cupboard in the daytime.

Major items of traditional furniture in such rooms will include a large wooden chest of drawers (**tansu**), which, as an heirloom, is often elaborately lacquered and decorated, and the folding screen (**byōbu**), unique to Japan, which can be set up instantly to screen off part of the room for privacy. Many of the elaborately decorated ones have become museum pieces.

Because of the rectangular mats made of thick rice straw (**tatami**), which allow living at floor level, a lot of traditional furniture is much lower than in the West, e.g. serving tables (**chabudai**), often with collapsible legs, and writing desks (**tsukue**). Chairs are rare, since you traditionally sit on thick cushions (**zabuton**) with your legs tucked under your body. Sometimes chairs with high backs were brought in for persons of high rank. These may also have armrests, but no legs. If there is a square hole in the **tatami**-covered floor over which the table has been placed (the so-called **hori-gotatsu** or sunken foot-warmer) Westerners can feel quite comfortable in such a chair, since the leg below the knee is warmed by a **hibachi** (charcoal brazier, these days electrically heated).

Traditionally, bamboo was used a lot for making furniture, while sliding doors (**fusuma**) are made from wooden frames with thick paper or cardboard covering, often beautifully decorated.

further (*distance*) motto tōi
 is that much further? motto tōi des ka?

future shōrai
 in future shōrai ni

FUTURE TENSE

Japanese has no separate future tense form. Instead, the present tense serves that function, so for example:

totemo yoi des

can mean:	that is very good
as well as:	that will be very good

Context and the use of 'time words' (tomorrow, next year etc.) make it clear that the speaker is talking about the future:

raishū Igirisu ni kaerimas
I shall return to England next week
[*literally: next week England to return*]

Sometimes, however, a plain present verb is used instead, followed by **deshō**, to indicate a supposition about the future:

raishū kaeru deshō
(I suppose) he'll be returning next week

kuji goro kuru deshō
(I expect) she'll come around nine o'clock

Remember, however, that **deshō** is not a future verb – it simply implies supposition on the part of the speaker. This is sometimes a supposition about the future, but may also involve other tenses:

senshū atta hito wa chūgoku-jin deshō
the man we met last week was probably Chinese

G

gap: a gap in the market shijō de no gyappu

garage (*for petrol and oil only*) gasorin-stando
(*car repairs as well*) garēji

garden niwa

garlic nin-niku

gas (*for cooker etc.*) gas

geisha girl geisha

GEISHA

Geisha can be defined as traditional highly skilled
female entertainers. They can be hired to offer
companionship to wealthy Japanese males in some
exclusive restaurants in Kyoto and Tokyo. This
involves traditional dancing, singing, playing games,
and erotically stimulating conversation. While num-
bering about 80,000 in the 1920s they are now down
to less than 17,000 and are far outnumbered by
hostesses working in Western-style cabarets and bars.

As opposed to the latter, **geisha** receive a long and
arduous training in the traditional arts. In spite of
some social prejudice, most Japanese tend to respect
them as being preservers of traditional art and
culture.

Contrary to superficial Western expectations, **geisha** are not primarily engaged to cater for the sexual
gratification of their male customers. Instead, being
very expensive to hire, they are mainly used by the
host to impress the other men at a party, implying
that he has great powers of sexual attraction, as well
as an exceedingly fat wallet.

GENDER

Japanese nouns do not have different forms to
indicate gender.

gents (*toilet*) toire 男

GESTURES

Since there was virtually no contact between Japan
and the West until just over a century ago, it is not
surprising that only a few gestures have exactly the
same meaning in both cultures. Conversely, some

gestures are shared, but their meaning is different. Finally, some Japanese gestures have no equivalent in the West.

Many Japanese gestures allow information to be conveyed in silence: it could well be rude if certain things were talked about and in crowded Japan you are easily overheard by others. Some of these gestures can be readily understood by Westerners, e.g. an invitation to a drinking party by miming the holding of a **sake** cup and performing a slight 'throw-away' motion with the wrist. Such a gesture is called **temane**, which can be translated as 'hand imitation'.

When a male vigorously scratches his head behind one ear, he shows that he is **komatta** (perplexed). Making an anti-clockwise circling motion with the index finger pointing towards the temple (**hidari-maki** to wind anti-clockwise) shows that the person referred to is thought of as crazy. Westerners also readily understand the gesture for 'I' or 'myself', where the index finger is pointed at one's nose (not at the chest).

Misunderstanding can occur with the following gestures: making a circle with the index finger and thumb traditionally refers to **o-kane** (money) in Japan, while in the West this is a sign for 'OK' or 'fine'. When Japanese hold both fists, one before the other, in front of the nose, they want to show that another person is over-confident.

Calling somebody towards oneself is achieved by extending the arm slightly, palm turned downwards, and fluttering the fingers. From a distance this can be interpreted by Westerners as waving good-bye – exactly the opposite of the effect intended.

The Western 'thumbs up' also has a different meaning in Japan – there it refers to some male, e.g. the boss, or a woman's boyfriend, lover, or husband. The sign complementary to this is unknown in the West, and considered a little rude in Japan: raising one's little finger up, which refers to somebody's girlfriend, mistress, or wife.

A fast crossing and re-crossing of the index fingers refers to sword fighting, and indicates that two persons are having a fight.

Instead of saying directly that somebody is lying, the gesture called **mayu-tsuba** ('eyebrow-saliva') can be used, where you briefly lick your index finger and then stroke it over an eyebrow. This movement was

originally a magic protection from foxes, who were
believed to have magical powers.

To refer to a female's jealousy, both hands can be
lifted to the forehead, index fingers sticking up and
angling forward. This represents a woman's 'horns
of jealousy'. Incidentally, these are the horns of
jealousy hidden on a bride's wedding day by her
white ceremonial headgear, called **tsuno-kakushi**
('horn-hider').

Finally, the hand waved limply in front of the
face, with the thumb nearest to it, indicates somebody's desire to pass closely in front of another
person. It is accompanied by one or several slight
bows.

On the whole, both British and Japanese are
relatively restrained with their gestures. Avoid
touching Japanese in public, and don't slap them on
the back or grab them by the arm when the
discussion gets animated.

get: where can I get . . .? . . . wa doko de te ni hairimas
ka?

have you got . . .? . . . o motte imas ka?

I haven't got . . . . . . o motte imasen

how do I get there? dō yatte, soko e ikemas ka?

how do I get to . . .? dō yatte, . . . e ikemas ka?

will you tell me when to get off? oriru toki ni
shirasete kudasaimas ka?

we'll get back to you on that sore ni tsuite, ato de
renraku shimas

gift purezento, okurimono

GIFTS

The exchange of appropriate gifts is a serious matter
in Japan. Its main purpose is to keep a relationship,
once begun, on an even keel. The function is not, as
it often is in the United States: 'Please take this – I
want to give you something (so that you like
me . . .)'. Gifts in Japan are, therefore, almost always
reciprocated by counter-gifts of closely matched
value at appropriate intervals.

So take care not to make your own gifts too
expensive, since you are forcing the recipient to
return something at the same level, which in turn
obligates you, ad infinitum. Try to check beforehand
with other Japanese acquaintances about the mon-

etary value a gift should have vis-à-vis specific persons.

As an outsider, you need not participate fully in this ritual, which to many Japanese is tiresome but unavoidable. Furthermore, some Japanese, knowing that you are a temporary visitor, may treat you more in a 'Western' way as regards gifts, i.e. casually.

Your gifts (especially when brought from abroad) will naturally be appreciated and will give rise to return gifts. It is worth remembering three major rules:

1. Japanese always wrap their gifts, expecting the same of you. The wrapping must be done with care, since it enhances the value of the gift. To Japanese it matters a lot whether the identical object is wrapped in the equivalent of Harrod's wrapping papers, as opposed to, say, the Japanese equivalent of Woolworths. Therefore, open Japanese gifts carefully and treat the paper itself with respect. When you need to have your own gifts wrapped, get the advice of a Japanese friend, or a department store, whose sales ladies may be induced to wrap those gifts you brought along with some further ones you can buy there. Fancy ribbons and paper can be obtained at the **bumbōgu-ya** (stationery shop) section of the same department store.

2. Once you have been offered a gift, you cannot refuse it without giving offence. However, if you suspect that it might be a bribe, e.g. possibly being much more valuable than is reasonably to be expected, you can violate rule 3 (by acting the 'dumb' foreigner), open it, and hand it back with, 'I am sorry, you seem to have made a mistake', if necessary.

3. In Japan, gifts are traditionally not opened in front of the giver. This permits both parties to save face, since the one offering the gift usually goes on at length about the worthlessness of the gift, and the receiving party insists that he/she cannot possibly accept such a valuable item (*see* POLITENESS LEVELS). However, young people and Westerners, especially if urged to do so, can open their gifts straight away.

Before your departure from Europe, try to buy a lot of relatively inexpensive gifts, typical of your home town or area. On occasion, even small and almost worthless items, such as picture postcards, will be appreciated as tokens for the kindness Westerners tend to receive in Japan. Whisky used to

be a popular gift, but with growing Japanese affluence, only high-quality boxed bottles or rare malt
whiskies retain some status. However, don't forget
the wives of your Japanese acquaintances: in that
case expensive Indian or Ceylon tea, which can be
shared by everyone, and is light, makes a good gift.

Should you run out of such gifts, the Japanese
department stores hold plenty in reserve for you –
though greatly overpriced.

giggle (*verb*) kusu-kusu warau /waraimas/

girl onna-no-ko

give ageru /agemas/
please give me . . . . . . o kudasai

GIVING

Since the act of giving may occur between people at
all social levels, it should come as no surprise to
learn that Japanese, with its tremendous attention to
status, has many different words for 'give', each with
overtones revealing the status of the giver vis-à-vis
the receiver, as well as the attitude of the speaker
and the status of the listener(s) vis-à-vis the speaker
and those being spoken about.

At its simplest, however, if you are doing the
giving, use **ageru/agemas/**:

> **I gave it to Mrs Otsumi**
> Otsumi-san ni agemashta

> **I gave it to my father**
> chichi ni agemashta

If someone gives you something, use **kudasaru
/kudasaimas/**:

> **the company president gave it to me**
> shācho ga kudasaimashta

Other common verbs include **sashiageru/sashia-
gemas/**, which is a politer form of **ageru**:

> **I'll give it to the president**
> shachō ni sashiagemas

and **kureru/kuremas/**, which is used when whoever it
is who gave you something is not superior to you or
is a member of your group:

> **Nozomu (junior) gave it to me**
> Nozomu-kun ga kureta

glass (*for drinking*) guras
(*material*) garas

glasses (*spectacles*) megane

gloves tebukuro

go iku /ikimas/
> **tomorrow I'm going to . . .** (*place*) ashta . . . e iku tsumori des
> **I went there yesterday** kinō soko e ikimashta
> **where are you going?** doko e iku no des ka?

Note that **iku** is never used if home is the place you are going to – in that case, use **kaeru**:
> **I'm going home**
> uchi ni kaerimas

gold kin

good ī
> **that's very good** (sore wa) totemo ī des

Note, however, that 'not good' is **yoku nai.**

goodbye (*formal*) sayōnara
(*informal*) dewa mata, ja mata

GOODBYE

While all phrase books on foreign languages will tell you how to say 'hello', few instruct you as to leave-taking. This can become rather irksome – not wanting to offend, you feel forced to stay on and on, not knowing what to say.

Your Japanese hosts are unlikely to say directly that some meeting is over. Instead, they might drop hints, such as, 'the taxi is waiting', etc. Acting on that hint, you can then say:
> **soro-soro o-itoma shimas**
> I'd better be getting going

Other useful expressions are:
> **go-chisō-sama deshta**
> it was delicious (*should food or any refreshments have been served*)
> **dōmo arigatō gozaimashta**
> thank you very much indeed

Remember that it sounds better if you utter some polite phrase in English, even if your partner(s) don't understand a word, than if you say nothing at all. The function of these many polite phrases, which also exist in English, but which are much more varied in Japanese, is not really transmission of specific information, but simply the message that you are grateful for (unspecified) favours received.

Finally, you can say the (for Westerners) ubiquitous

sayōnara
goodbye

which is strictly speaking only said when taking
leave for a long time, tinged with sadness that one
might never see each other again. Among Japanese,
a more common farewell is:

dewa mata
well then, see you again

If you know that you are meeting again the next day,
you can add the equivalent of 'tomorrow':

dewa mata ashta
see you tomorrow

If offered a hand, shake it lightly; otherwise two or
more light bows will do.

goods shinamono

government seifu

grateful: we're very grateful totemo kansha shte imas

great (*tremendous*) subarashī
that's really great! hontō ni subarashī des!

green midori iro (no)

GREEN
Certain items commonly referred to as green in
English may be translated into Japanese by **aoi**
(blue). The two principal examples are vegetation
and traffic lights:

green grass
aokusa, aoi shiba
green vegetation
aoi kusaki
green light
aoshingō

green tea o-cha

grey hai-iro (no)

ground tochi

ground floor ikkai
Note that the Japanese system parallels the American one, their first floor being our ground floor,
their second floor being our first floor etc.

guarantee (*noun*) hoshō
there's a one-year guarantee ichinen hoshō des

guest (*plain form*) kyaku

When talking to a guest or when talking about a guest of high status the honorifics **o-** and **-sama** are added to form the word **o-kyaku-sama**.

GUESTS

Although Japanese are very hospitable, it is relatively rare for visitors from abroad to be invited to their homes. Instead, they are likely to be wined and dined in a most expensive fashion in public restaurants.

However, if you are invited, regard it as a great honour and try to remember the following:

Take along a suitable gift (ideally one from your home town – *see* GIFTS).

Make sure that you have the proper directions for your taxi – or try to be met at the nearest railway station. As these are sometimes very crowded, and since there may be several exits, it might be worth agreeing with your host that you simply stay put on the platform on alighting, say, at the very front (or the very back) end of the train to be met there.

On being ushered into the house, remember to take off your shoes and use the slippers provided. However, before stepping onto **tatami** mats, the slippers are discarded as well and your journey proceeds in stockinged feet. On entering the toilet, use the extra toilet slippers, if provided, and don't forget to change back to your 'regular' slippers when exiting. If the toilet is Japanese-style, you will have to squat down, with your face towards the water container, not the door, uncomfortable but hygienic.

Should you be invited to sit in a Japanese-style room, squatting on the floor, remember that males are allowed to sit cross-legged, while females may fold the legs under their bodies on sitting down, and then move their weight off to one side. Legless chairs with backs and sunken foot-warmers (**horigotatsu**) can be a great relief on such occasions – *see* FURNITURE.

Since conversation is likely to dry up at some point, it may be a good idea to take along photos of your home town, house, relatives etc.

Conversely, you can always request to be instructed in the art of paper folding (**origami**), which all Japanese learn to do in childhood. Remember that in a relaxed atmosphere, child-like amusements are perfectly acceptable, even when the youngest member of the party already has grey hairs.

Some useful words and phrases:

First of all you are likely to hear:

please come in
dōzo o-agari kudasai

You might well want to say:

sorry to have kept you waiting
o-machi-dō-sama deshta

I'm sorry that I'm late
osoku natte, sumimasen

are you well?
o-genki des ka?

I am well, thanks for asking
genki des, o-kage-sama de

you have a very nice home
ī o-sumai des, ne

please take it (*the gift*)
shitsurei des ga, dōzo
[*literally: I'm being rude, but please take it*]

thanks (*also said at the start of a meal*)
itadakimas

Your host might say:

Nihongo ga o-jōzu des, ne!
you speak Japanese very well!

To which you can reply:

īe, mada des
no, not yet

Note that Japanese do not tend to praise people or things directly, with one exception: your excellent(!) command of Japanese will be praised by all and sundry if you are a short-term visitor.

guidebook ryokō annai-sho

H

hair kami-no-ke

haircut sampatsu

hairdresser's bi-yō-in
   Pronounce this word carefully: the similar sounding
   b'yō-in means 'hospital'!

half hambun
   half each hambun zutsu
   half a kilo go-hyaku guramu
   half an hour san-juppun
   See TIME

hand te

hand baggage te-nimotsu

handbag handobaggu

handkerchief hankachi

HANDKERCHIEFS
As in the United States, handkerchiefs have largely
been replaced by paper tissues for blowing one's
nose. Even then, tissues are not much used in
public, and on days when the flu is rampant, loud
sniffling noises can be heard everywhere. In such
cases, gauze masks (**masku**) are often worn in front
of the mouth – a custom which dates from the great
flu epidemic of 1918.
   If you absolutely must blow your nose, try to get
out of earshot of the assembled company (admittedly
often difficult!), or, at the very least, turn away as
discreetly as possible.
   But handkerchiefs are very important in Japan for
drying one's hands after washing them in public
washrooms, since drying facilities are often absent.
And Japanese women use their handkerchiefs to fan
themselves on hot days, to pat their face, and as a
napkin to put on their lap when eating in a
restaurant.

HANDS – HOLDING HANDS
Emotions are rarely shown in public – be it love or
dislike. Although nobody in the vicinity might seem
to mind, remember that a female Japanese friend
will get a bad name for open displays of affection. If

you want to hold hands (and more) – do it discreetly, like the Japanese, and patronize one of the many **dōhan kissaten** [*literally: 'go-together coffee shops'*], where the backs of the chairs are high and the other customers are far too busy with *their* hand-holding, etc., to notice you. You might even suggest a visit to one of the exotic **rabu hoteru** ('love hotels') or **abekku hoteru** ('avec hotel' – from the French 'with') where you will come across the utmost discretion on the part of the management.

hanging scroll kakejiku

happy ureshī
   we're not happy with . . . . . . dewa, ureshku arimasen

hard (*difficult*) muzukashī

hat bōshi

have motsu /motte imas/
   can I have . . .? (*please give me*) . . . o o-negai shimas (*or* . . . o kudasai)
   I don't have . . . . . . o motte imasen
   do you have . . .? . . . o motte imas ka?
   he has . . . (kare wa) . . . o motte imas
   we have . . . . . . o motte imas
   do they have . . .? (karera wa) . . . o motte imas ka?
   I have to . . . . . . -nakereba narimasen (*see* **must**)
   I have to go tomorrow ashta ikanakereba narimasen

he kare
   he's American kare wa Amerika-jin des
   he's paying kare ga haraimas

HE

Personal pronouns like **kare** are not considered very polite if used in direct reference to a person present or to anyone due respect. Politer phrases such as:

> **kono kata**
> this person

are sometimes used, but frequently the person's title will be used instead. For example, if a telephone call comes for Mr Yasunaga, managing director, who is not in that day, the company employee is likely to answer that:

> **shachō wa kyō o-yasumi des**
> the managing director is not here today
> [*literally: managing director as-for today away is*]

rather than **kare wa . . .** (*see* PERSONAL PRONOUNS).

head atama

headache zutsū

health kenkō
your very good health! go-kenkō o shukushte, kampai!
See TOASTS

hear kiku /kikimas/
I can't hear kikoemasen

heart (*poetical, emotional*) kokoro
(*medical term*) shinzō

heavy omoi

heel kakato

hello (*on telephone*) moshi-moshi!

HELLO

There is no single word that can adequately translate the general English greeting 'hello'. The translation often given is:

kon-nichi wa

(also equated with 'good afternoon'), which can actually be heard any time from mid-morning to early evening, when **komban wa** ('good evening') takes over. However, **kon-nichi wa** is crucially different from 'hello' in two major respects:

1. Once it has been said to a person, it cannot be used again until the following day; indeed it should not be used if **ohayō gozaimas** (good morning) was the greeting given earlier.

2. Unlike **ohayō**, **kon-nichi wa** is never used by members of the same family to each other; in fact it is usually not even exchanged by people working in the same office, who will often prefer some other expression such as **ohayō gozaimas** (good morning), **yā, okurete shimatte** (sorry to be late) or **kyō wa atsui des ne!** (it's hot today, isn't it?)

Other possibilities exist such as simple vocalizations like:

ā, Okada-san
hello, Mr Okada

or:

oss! (*used by martial arts devotees*)

or simply a bowing of the head or a smile.

help (*noun*) taske
 help! taskete!

her (*possessive adjective*) kanojo no
 (*pronoun*) **I saw her** kanojo o mimashta
 I'll give it to her kanojo ni agemas
 I'll phone her kanojo ni denwa shimas
 See PERSONAL PRONOUNS

here koko

hers kanojo no
 it's hers kanojo no des

high (*hill, costs*) takai

hill oka

him: I saw him kare o mimashta
 I'll give it to him kare ni agemas
 I'll phone him kare ni denwa shimas
 See PERSONAL PRONOUNS

hire (*car*) kariru /karimas/
 I want to hire a car kuruma o karitai des

his (*adjective and pronoun*) kare no
 is that his bag? sore wa kare no kaban des ka?
 is that his? sore wa kare no des ka?
 See POSSESSIVE ADJECTIVES

hole ana

holiday (*vacation, public*) yasumi

HOLIDAYS
Most Japanese take only a very short vacation from
their work. So they have to make the most of set
public holidays. Apart from the many local festivals,
Japan has the following national holidays:

1 January	New Year's Day
15 January	Coming of Age Day
12 February	National Foundation Day
21 or 22 March	Vernal Equinox Day
29 April	Green Day
3 May	Constitution Memorial Day
5 May	Children's Day
15 September	Respect for the Aged Day
23 or 24 September	Autumnal Equinox Day
10 October	Sports Day
3 November	Culture Day

| 23 November | Labour Thanksgiving Day |
| 23 December | Emperor's Birthday |

Christmas is not a national holiday, although many parties – called **bōnen-kai** ('forget the year') – are held from then onwards until New Year's Eve. Over New Year many shops and offices remain closed for three or four days. Avoid travelling long distances during this period as one in two Japanese seem to want to do the same. Long-distance travel during the so-called 'Golden Week' (29 April – 5 May) should also be avoided since this period contains three public holidays, which allows many people to take the whole week off.

home (*my own*) uchi
    (*yours*) o-taku
    (*neutral*) katei, ie [ee-eh]
    at home (*any of the above, plus*) . . . de
    at your home o-taku de
    the home market kokunai shijō

HOME

The Japanese home is a very private place. Few people except close kin are invited inside, for this means that full hospitality must be offered. Instead, visitors are often met and entertained in nearby coffee shops, or advance no further than the ubiquitous **genkan** – an entrance hall not quite inside, but not outside either. It is here at this half-way point that one is asked to take off one's shoes and is provided with slippers, before being urged:

    o-agari kudasai
    please step up

if invited in (*see* GUEST).

This simple act, like so many others in Japan, is both physical and psychological, transforming one from outsider to insider. This is the demarcation line between the private and the outside world.

If you are not invited in, you can stand in the **genkan** and deliver your message while keeping your shoes on. Some reasons for the fact that Westerners are not easily invited into the home are: (1) it is considered too small and untidy; (2) they might feel uncomfortable sitting on the floor or using a squat toilet; (3) the housewife may be embarrassed having to speak English.

hope: I hope so sō da to ī des ne
   I hope not sō ja nai to ī des ne

horrible osoroshī

hospital b'yō-in

hospitality motenashi
   thank you for your hospitality motenashte itadaite
   dōmo arigatō

HOSPITALITY

Towards guests, especially if they are Westerners, Japanese tend to be very hospitable (*see* BILLS, GIFTS, HOST). For top company employees there are generous expense accounts to entertain clients, but even in the private sphere hospitality can sometimes be overwhelming. Being accorded VIP treatment is not everyone's cup of tea, since it can severely limit one's own choice of movements. It may therefore be useful to let your hosts know right at the outset that you plan to visit others as well during your stay so as to give yourself some freedom of movement.

When departing from one's hosts, Westerners tend to express their gratitude for the pleasant time they enjoyed, but Japanese are accustomed to apologize for having taken the hosts' time. Thus, on leave-taking, they will tend to say:

   o-jikan o torimashta
   I'm sorry I took your time

or:

   o-jama shimashta
   I'm sorry I disturbed you

These are used in conjunction with expressions of thanks for the food:

   go-chisō-sama deshta
   it was a feast

As a Westerner you might be hesitant to apologize, so the last-mentioned phrase should be sufficient, together with:

   go-shinsetsu ni arigatō gozaimashta
   many thanks for your kindness

A point to remember is that, on meeting again at a later date, Japanese rarely fail to thank their former hosts by saying:

   kono aida wa dōmo arigatō gozaimashta
   thanks a lot for the other day

or by 'apologizing' once again:

senjitsu wa shitsurei itashimashta
I was rude the other day

host shujin-yaku

HOST

It is very hard to reciprocate Japanese hospitality exactly, as regards either money or personal commitment. This causes many Westerners in Japan to feel perpetually guilty, or scared that one day the munificent Japanese hosts might appear on their poor doorstep in the West.

For one thing, 'to go Dutch' (**warikan ni shimas**) is relatively rare among Japanese, except for students. Invitations, however, must be reciprocated, since the balance should be preserved (*see* GIFTS). While in Japan, an occasional return invitation to a Western restaurant may be appropriate – but that can be very expensive. If you have to entertain a large group of people you can stick to Western customs and invite them all to a cocktail party. In such cases, you are a Western host and behave in a polite way similar to that found in your home country. Don't forget to reciprocate on return to Europe by sending 'thank you' gifts, such as calendars, or photo books of your city or area. Such responsibility for saying 'thank you' does not necessarily stay confined to one person in Japanese eyes: in the case of a young Western student who had enjoyed the hospitality of a Japanese family, the latter were somewhat peeved to receive letters of thanks from the student only – they had expected one from the parents as well.

hot atsui
  (*spicy*) karai
The Japanese have a special phrase for hot water: **oyu**. Note that a literally translated phrase like **atsui mizu** is very strange indeed.

hotel hoteru　ホテル

HOTELS

Since space is limited in Japan, hotel accommodation tends to be expensive. For something equivalent to Western tastes see BUSINESS HOTEL. International hotels are marvellous – provided somebody else picks up the bill! Japanese-style inns are called **ryokan** and also tend to be expensive because of the large staff needed to keep the customers contented. They usually include two meals (Japanese style). Get in touch with the town's tourist office or **kankō-annaijo** for advice on the choice of a hotel.

hour jikan
 in an hour ato ichi-jikan de
 See TIME

house (*building*) ie
 See HOME

how dō
 how are you? o-genki des ka?
 how long? (*distance*) dono kurai no des ka?
 (*time in hours*) nan-jikan kakarimas ka?
 how long does it take? (*journey etc.*) dono kurai kakarimas ka?
 how many? ikutsu des ka?
 how much? ikura des ka?
 how do you do? kon-nichi wa?

HOW DO YOU DO?

After introducing yourself to someone for the first time by saying:

> **hajimemashte – X des – dōzo yoroshku**
> glad to meet you – I am X – how do you do?

you can say:

> **o-genki des ka?**
> how are you?

To which the reply is:

> **okagesama de, genki des**
> yes, I am well, thanks

humour yūmoa

HUMOUR

Bawdy humour has been relished in Japan since ancient days, especially since there was no Christianity to make it look 'sinful'. In fact, the myths concerning Japan's origin specifically refer to bawdy humour. The Sun Goddess Amaterasu was lured out of her cave by a lascivious dance. She had hidden there after a quarrel with the other gods, thereby plunging the world into darkness. To entice her to return, a strip-tease dance was staged in front of her cave. Curious why all the other gods should be roaring with laughter, she finally relented and came out, and the world was filled with light again.

Such humour, often with very explicit sexual themes, was to be found widely among peasant men and women before the Second World War. However, since that time the ethics of status-conscious 'polite society', as well as Western missionary disgust and Japanese attempts to look 'presentable' in the eyes of disapproving Westerners, have caused such humour to go largely underground, and the cruder versions are to be found in present-day sex comics read avidly by many Japanese men on commuter trains.

More important is the social satire which makes fun of those big-wigs who are weaklings at heart. However, owing to the importance of 'keeping face', few living persons are directly lampooned this way – the humour aims more at pompous people in general. Thus satirical newspaper cartoons which take the mickey out of actual politicians and bureaucrats are almost completely absent. With the ever-present need to use honorific expressions to or about one's seniors, while humbling oneself (*see* POLITE-NESS LEVELS), life is rarely relaxed enough to call the whole system into question by laughing at it. Neither is self-deprecating humour very common in Japan, although making a fool of yourself on TV shows is becoming more popular.

Therefore beware of making jokes about others, even if such jokes may seem rather innocent in English.

Another area of humour is that of punning. Since Japanese has many words which are pronounced exactly alike, but which may have a totally different meaning, the language lends itself to puns.

This fact of the language also gives rise to some superstitions. For example, the sea bream (**tai**) is often eaten at celebratory banquets because its name happens to coincide with the last two syllables of **medetai** (joyous, auspicious); similarly, no hospital will have a room No. 4, since one reading of the character for four is **shi** – which also means 'death' (which is why four is often pronounced **yon** instead).

hungry onaka ga suita
  I'm hungry onaka ga suite imas
  I'm not very hungry onaka ga suite imasen

hurry: hurry! isogi-nasai!
  there's no hurry isogu hitsuyō wa arimasen

hurt: it hurts itai des
   it doesn't hurt itakunai des

husband (*one's own*) shujin
   (*polite*) go-shujin
   (*neutral*) otto

HUSBANDS

As in the case of the word for 'wife', there are many
words to choose from, depending on the specific
situation. The neutral word is:

   otto

When speaking to others about one's own husband:

   shujin

or:

   danna

is used, but polite prefixes or suffixes are added
when speaking about somebody else's husband:

   go-shujin, danna-san, danna-sama

I

I

The masculine form for 'I' (when used) is **watakshi**,
watashi, **boku** or **ore** – in descending order of
politeness. The feminine form is **atakshi** or **atashi**.
See PERSONAL PRONOUNS.

ice kōri
with ice (*e.g. coffee*) ais kōhī

ice cream aiskurīm
chocolate ice cream chokorēto aiskurīm
vanilla ice cream banira aiskurīm

if moshi

IF

With the word **moshi** you use the **-ra** form of the
verb, which is made by adding this suffix to a past
tense (either plain or polite: *see* VERBS):

> **if it rains**
> moshi ame ga futtara

> **if you went early**
> moshi hayaku ittara

ill b'yōki
I feel ill b'yōki no yō des

immediately sugu ni

IMPERATIVES

Although there are true command forms in Japanese, they are felt to be very brusque and impolite.
You are unlikely to come across them, except when
hearing army commands in old war films like *Tenko*.
In polite conversation, Japanese tend to order and
request in roundabout ways, such as, 'wouldn't you
like to . . .?' etc. One mild imperative form is **kudasai**
(to grant, to condescend to), which is attached to the
participle (*see* VERBS).

> **please show me your passport**
> paspōto o misete kudasai
> [*literally: passport (object) show please*]

This can be intensified by prefixing the sentence with **dōzo** (please):

> **dōzo paspōto o misete kudasai**

Whereas **kudasai** implies the granting of a favour, a more direct request (though still polite) is to use **nasai** with the basic stem (*see* VERBS):

> **show me your passport**
> paspōto o mise-nasai

In this case **dōzo** is not added.

For negative commands, the verb in question is the plain negative present plus **-de** and it is again followed by **kudasai**:

> **don't show them the passport!**
> paspōto o mise-naide kudasai

Some common phrases:

> **please stop at the hotel!**
> hoteru de tomatte kudasai
> [*literally: hotel at stopping please*]

> **stop (doing) it!**
> yame-nasai
> [*literally: discontinuing please*]

> **please don't bother!**
> kamawanaide kudasai
> [*literally: not bothering please*]

import (*verb*) yu-nyū suru

important taisetsu (na)
  it is important (sore wa) taisetsu des

impossible fukanō (na)

in . . . . . . no naka ni
  in the box hako no naka ni
  in Japan Nihon ni/de wa
  in Japanese Nihongo de
  in my room heya no naka ni/de
  in two weeks from now ato nishūkan de

IN

When 'in' refers to the location of an object (i.e. where it is), the particle **ni** is used:

> **it's in the box**
> hako no naka ni arimas

> **he's in the office**
> jimusho ni imas

However, when 'in' refers to the location of an activity, the particle used is **de**:

> **he's working in his office**
> jimusho de hataraite imas
>
> **I was studying in the library**
> toshokan de benkyō shimashta

included: is . . . included? . . . wa fukumarete imas ka?

inflation (*money*) infurēshon

information jōhō

information office annaijo

instant coffee instanto kōhī

insurance hoken

interesting omoshiroi
> **that's very interesting** (sore wa) totemo omoshiroi des

international koksai-teki (na)

international driving licence koksai jidōsha menkyoshō

interpret tsūyaku suru /tsūyaku shimas/
> **could you please interpret?** tsūyaku shte kudasaimas ka?

interpreter tsūyaku
> **we need an interpreter** tsūyaku ga hitsuyō des

introduce: may I introduce . . . ? . . . -san o go-shōkai itashimas?
See BUSINESS CARDS, HOW DO YOU DO?, MEET

invitation shōtai
> **thank you for the invitation** go-shōtai o arigatō gozaimas

INVITATIONS

The role you should play after having accepted an invitation is discussed under GUESTS and GIFTS. Japanese will extend invitations to you, usually to some place in town, but rarely to their home. The reasons for this are given under HOME. Suitable phrases to use when having accepted somebody's invitation are discussed under HOSPITALITY and HOST. But here are some more:

> **may I invite you to a meal?**
> moshi yorosh-kattara, shokuji ni kite kudasai?
>
> **yes, I accept with pleasure**
> hai, yorokonde

sorry, I can't make it
zannen-nagara, ikemasen

invite shōtai suru
Usually seniors invite juniors and locals invite visitors. After that a return invitation is in order – *see* BILLS, GIFTS, GUESTS, HOST.

invoice (*noun*) okurijō

Ireland Airurando

Irish (*adjective*) Airurando no
I'm Irish Airurando-jin des

iron (*for clothes*) airon
(*metal*) tetsu
could you please get these ironed? (kore ni) airon o kakete kudasaimas ka?

is *see* BE

island shima

it: it is . . . sore wa . . . des
is it . . .? . . . des ka?

IT

Japanese doesn't really have a word for 'it', so in translation it usually just disappears:

where is it?
doko des ka?
[*literally: where is (question word)*]

there it is
asoko des
[*literally: over here is*]

who is it?
donata des ka?
[*literally: who is (question word)*]

it's Mrs Otsumi
Otsumi-san des
[*literally: Mrs Otsumi is*]

is it hot?
atsui des ka
[*literally: hot is (question word)*]

The word **sore** is sometimes found instead, but this is a demonstrative pronoun rather than a personal pronoun and is closer to our word 'that':

what is it?
sore wa nan des ka?

A sentence like:

it's very cheap

could perhaps be translated as:

sore wa totemo yasui des

but just:

totemo yasui des

would be more natural.

The tag questions '. . . is it?' and '. . . isn't it?' are both covered by the simple word **ne**, said usually with a drop in pitch:

it's no good, is it?
yoku arimasen, ne

it's very good, isn't it?
totemo ī des ne?

J

jacket jaketto
   See CLOTHES

jam (*for bread*) jamu

January ichi-gatsu

Japan Nihon　日本

Japan Sea Nihonkai

Japanese (*adjective*) Nihon no
   (*person*) Nihon-jin
   (*language*) Nihongo
   in Japanese Nihongo de
   See WRITING SYSTEM

Japanese-style wafū

Japanese-style hotel ryokan

jetlag: I'm/he's suffering from jetlag jisa-boke des

jewellery hōseki

job (*work*) shigoto
   what's your job? (anata no) o-shigoto wa nan des ka?
   if we get this job (*order*) moshi kono shigoto o hiki-
   uketara . . .

joint venture gōbengaisha [= joint venture company]

joke (*noun*) jōdan
   you're joking! jōdan deshō!

journey ryokō
   safe journey! anzen na ryokō o!

July shichi-gatsu

June roku-gatsu

just (*only*) . . . dake
   just one hitotsu dake
   just a little bit hon no skoshi dake

K

keep: please keep it dōzo o-mochi kudasai
    keep the change o-tsuri wa irimasen

key kagi
    the key for room number . . . . . . gō shitsu no kagi

kilo kiro

kilometre kiromētoru

kind: that's very kind of you go-shinsetsu ni dōmo
arigatō
    what kind of . . . ? dono shurui no . . . ?

kiss (*noun*) kis

KISSING
The days when Rodin's famous statue 'The Kiss'
had to be specially kept behind screens during an
exhibition of the master's works in Tokyo have long
since gone. However, kissing in public is rarely seen,
and would certainly be severely frowned upon.
Walking hand-in-hand is about as far as it goes in
public. However, what goes on behind closed doors
is anybody's business – *see* HANDS – HOLDING HANDS.

In any case, kissing has far stronger erotic conno-
tations than in the West. Social kissing, e.g. of one's
children, relatives or friends, is unknown in Japan,
and mothers don't kiss their babies much in public,
either. However, erotic films, for a largely male
audience, feature much erotic kissing as a prelude to
still more intimate things and show that kissing is
rated as much more titillating than in the West.

As with so many other things in Japan, kissing
exists in its 'proper' place, for example in the private
rooms of 'love hotels', but the casual visitor, not
knowing where to look, will not find it, nor will most
Japanese be very helpful in the search.

kitchen daidokoro

knee hiza

knife (*Western*) naifu
    (*Japanese*) hōchō
    can I have a knife and fork, please? naifu to fōku o
o-negai shimas

KNIVES
Knives are not often used at table – *see* EATING
HABITS.

know shiru /shitte imas/
   I don't know shirimasen
   I know him kare o shitte imas
   I don't know him kare o shirimasen
   I didn't know that sore o shirimasen deshta
   I knew him kare o shitte imashta
   do you know where it is? doko ni aru ka shitte imas
   ka?

Korea Kankoku

L

ladies (*toilet*) toire 女
lady josei
lamb (*food*) ramu
lane (*narrow street*) komichi
language kotoba
large ōkī
last saigo (no)
    last week sen shū
    last night saku-ya
    last year kyonen
    the last time we met kono mae atta no wa

LATE

There are two common words used for expressing lateness. The first is the adjective **osoi**, which tends to imply late in the sense of 'not early'. For example:

    at a late hour
    osoi jikan ni

It is often used in its adverbial form **osoku**:

    till late at night
    yoru osoku made

    I won't be back until late
    osoku made kaerimasen

Note also, by the way, that **osoi** means 'slow'.

The other word for 'late' is the verb **okureru /okuremas/**, meaning 'to be late' in the sense of 'later than expected, arranged, promised, etc.':

    I'm sorry I'm late
    okurete sumimasen

    don't be late
    okurenaide kudasai

    she was half an hour late
    hanjikan okuremashta

    delivery will be about two weeks late
    haitatsu wa nishūkan gurai okuremas

In Japan, late deliveries should be avoided at all costs. These are viewed much more seriously in Japan and cause great embarrassment and loss of face to one's Japanese importer or distributor.

later ato de
    I'll come back later ato de modorimas

laugh (*verb*) warau /waraimas/

LAUGHTER

As in all other cultures, Japanese smile and laugh when they are happy. However, in Japan, expressions of seeming mirth are also used to hide embarrassment, perplexity, or anger – *see* FACIAL EXPRESSIONS. In the West we also tend to giggle nervously at times, especially when in our teens.

    There are many Japanese words imitating the sound of various kinds of laughter, for example:

to chuckle	kusu-kusu warau
to simper or grin	niya-niya warau
to guffaw	gera-gera warau
to laugh loudly	kara-kara warau

    To be laughed at in Japan is a very serious matter, since it implies 'losing face'. Beware of making jokes at the expense of other Japanese: while this can be very funny in Britain, it does not go down at all well in Japan; *see* HUMOUR.

law hōritsu

lawyer bengoshi

learn narau /naraimas/
    (*study*) benkyō suru /shimas/
    I'd like to learn Japanese Nihongo o naraitai des
    I'd like to study Japanese Nihongo o benkyō shitai des

leave (*depart*) tatsu /tachimas/
    I'm leaving in the morning asa tatsu tsumori des
    when does the plane leave? hikōki wa, itsu tachimas ka?

left hidari
    on the left hidari ni

left luggage (*office*) ichiji azukari-jo

leg ashi

less (*in quantity*) motto skunai
    less than a year ichinen inai ni

letter (*mail*) tegami

letter of credit shōmei-sho shin-yō-jō

letterbox yūbin-bako　ポスト

LETTERS

Until fairly recently, the style used in letters differed quite significantly from spoken Japanese. Although this has changed to a large degree, there is still more of the 'I remain, sir, your obedient servant' flavour remaining, which one naturally has to know about in detail. It seems that many Westerners, although good at the spoken language, will not venture further and write letters in Japanese as well, all the more so since educated Japanese are quite good at deciphering letters written in English. Sometimes it may be worth while writing one's letter in English and then stating that an answer in Japanese will also be fine. At that point one will of course have to find a Japanese friend to help with the translation, but it does allow the Japanese addressee to respond freely.

As can be expected, Japanese letters, even official ones, are not as abrupt as those in the West. Even when writing in English, it will, therefore, not come amiss if the introductory paragraph concerns itself with something general, such as the recipient's state of health, the weather etc. The recipient should also be thanked for things done in the past before coming to the main point of the letter.

When addressing Japanese (using English), one can either use Mr/Mrs/Miss and family name, or the family name followed by **-san** (*see* FIRST NAMES).

When writing, say, to Mr NOGUCHI (surname) Takao (given name) the letter can start either:

Dear Noguchi-san,

or:

Dear Mr Noguchi,

The suffix **-san** is useful if you are not sure if the addressee is male or female, since it can be used for both. When writing personal letters, Japanese customarily use at least two sheets of paper, possibly because it may look rude to write only a short note. If only one sheet is covered with writing, the second, blank sheet is included nevertheless. This custom does not extend to business correspondence, and may also be disregarded when writing in English. *See also* ADDRESSES.

lift (*elevator*) erebētā

light (*electric*) denki
   (*not dark colour*) usui
   (*bright*) akarui

(*not heavy*) karui
  do you have a light? hi o kashte kuremasen ka?
  the light is not working denki wa tsukimasen

like: **I'd like a . . . . . .** ga hoshī des
  would you like a . . . ? . . . ga hoshī des ka?
  I like it sore ga ski des
  I don't like it sore ga ski dewa arimasen
  he likes it (kare wa) sore ga ski des
  he doesn't like it (kare wa) sore ga ski dewa arimasen
  like this kono yō ni

litre rittoru

little (*small*) chīsai
  a little skoshi
  a little sugar skoshi no satō

live sumu /sumimas/
  I live in . . . . . . ni sunde imas

loan words gairai-go

LOAN WORDS

It has been estimated that more than one third of commonly used Japanese words came as loan words from China from about 600 AD onwards. In this tendency Japanese resembles English, which likewise took over thousands of Greek, Latin and French loan words. Here many concepts can be expressed in at least two different ways: to think/to cogitate, to walk/to perambulate etc.

These Chinese loan words have become so deeply embedded in everyday Japanese speech that they are no longer thought of as foreign words. In dictionaries which give readings of Chinese characters (**kanji**), the pronunciation for each one is usually given in both **on-yomi** (Chinese reading) and **kun-yomi** (Japanese reading). For example, the Chinese character for the concept 'burning' 焼 can be read as **shō**, usually as the first character in a combination of two, as in 焼死 **shōshi** (death by fire). This is a pronunciation originally derived from Chinese. Alternatively, the identical character can be pronounced as the first syllable of 焼ける **yakeru** or 焼く **yaku** (the original Japanese word for 'burning'), and in this combination it forms nouns which are usually less abstract than those made up of Chinese-derived readings, such as 焼鳥 **yaki-tori** (grilled chicken).

After the opening-up of Japan to the outside world 120 years ago it first became fashionable to coin new words from Chinese-derived syllables. For example:

telephone
den-wa [*literally: electric talk*]

However, since the sixteenth century more and more Western loan words have entered the country, first from the Portuguese and Dutch languages, later almost exclusively from English. This has now become such a torrent of new words that it is hard for Japanese to keep up in all areas of life.

Such foreign loan words are almost exclusively written in the syllabic system called **katakana** (*see* WRITING SYSTEM), so that they stand out against the original Japanese and Chinese-derived words. Even the word for bread (**pan**, from the Portuguese 'pão') is still written in **katakana** after 400 years of use in the Japanese language, making it quite clear to every reader that it was something not indigenous to Japan.

While some Japanese lament this influx of foreign words and try (unsuccessfully) to stem the tide – rather in the same way as many French Academicians are trying to limit the intrusion of English loan words – others are quite happy, for the following reason: since such loan words are being used so freely for any new concept appearing in daily life, they do not make it necessary for any near-equivalent Japanese words to be put to use, forcing the latter to change their meaning. When after some time – whether a year, ten years, or a century – the foreign loan word is perhaps no longer needed, it can quietly disappear, having left the original stock of Japanese words unaffected.

It should be added that, whereas the influx of Chinese long ago did have some influence on the sentence structure of Japanese, Western languages present no such danger. In fact, it is Japanese grammar which often changes the foreign loan words, so that the latter frequently become all but unintelligible to native English speakers, and a special foreign loan-word dictionary has to be consulted to explain the words' origins and exact writing in Japanese.

Sometimes academics do not even bother to 'Japanize' the foreign words they want to boast with, but use them in their natural state to give a more 'learned' feeling to their paper. The following is a translation from a speech by a Japanese professor in

Japanese, trying to be profound, where several words (here printed in capital letters) were left in the original:

'On the question of COOPERATION in this matter, we would be prepared for MITARBEIT if both sides were on an EQUAL FOOTING. The EQUAL FOOTING is only NOMINAL, however, and DE FACTO. One side is CARDINAL and the other is COMPLEMENTAL, and we cannot expect success.'

Counts of **gairai-go** (loan words) in daily newspapers have shown that while in 1935 there appeared, on average, sixty Western loan words per page of Japan's largest daily newspaper, this had risen to an average of 173 after the Second World War.

Some examples of foreign loan words in Japanese:

Japanese pronunciation	Real spelling	English meaning
PORTUGUESE		
botan	*botão*	button
buranko	*balanço*	swing (at playground)
kastera	*abóbora de castella*	sponge cake
pan	*pão*	bread
tabako	*tabaco*	cigarette
totan	*tutanaga*	sheet zinc
DUTCH		
buriki	*blik*	tin
pinto	*brandpunt*	focus (camera lens)
randoseru	*ransel*	knapsack
GERMAN		
arerugī	*Allergie*	allergy
arubaito	*Arbeit*	part-time work
gebaruto (*or* **geba**)	*Gewalt*	violence, power (especially students')
kapseru	*Kapsel*	capsule
rebā	*Leber*	liver
tēma	*Thema*	theme
FRENCH		
abekku	*avec*	together
ankēto	*enquête*	questionnaire
bifuteki	*bifteck*	beef steak

konkūru	*concours*	contest
shikku	*chic*	chic
shūkurīm	*chou à la crème*	cream puffs
(*see* FOOD)		

ITALIAN

adajio	*adagio*	adagio
pianishimo	*pianissimo*	pianissimo
gondora	*gondola*	gondola

RUSSIAN

ikura	*ikra*	salmon roe
seiuchi	*sivuch*	walrus
wokka	*vodka*	vodka

There are thousands of English-derived loan words. For example:

apāto	a flat; block of flats
bā	bar
bōnas	bonus
būmu	boom
chāmingu	charming
doa	door
erochikku	erotic
handobaggu	handbag
imēji	image
kone	connection (personal)
masu-komi	mass communications
nansensu	nonsense
ofu reko	off the record
uīkuendo	weekend
yunīku	unique

But it is worth noting that the Japanese themselves, especially their advertising agencies, are busy making up English-sounding words which do not exist outside Japan, in order to give a spurious 'foreign' atmosphere to certain products. Here are some examples:

Japanese pronunciation	*Real spelling*	*English meaning*
appu heyā	*up hair*	swept-up, pompadour
bēsu appu	*base up*	increase (in salary)
gasorin stando	*gasoline stand*	petrol station

kanningu	*cunning*	cheating (in exams)
manmosu	*mammoth*	gigantic
nyū fēsu	*new face*	newly famous film actor
ōrudo misu	*old miss*	spinster
rasuto hebi	*last heavy*	final spurt
ribaibaru būmu	*revival boom*	traditional things coming back into fashion
romansu gurei	*romance grey*	middle-aged man's attractive grey hair
sararī man	*salary man*	salaried person
saido wāku	*side work*	part-time work
shatō	*chateau*	apartment block
wan man kā	*one man car*	bus with driver only
chī pī ō	*T.P.O.*	time, place, occasion (i.e. the proper 'T.P.O.' for drinking an expensive whisky)

If foreign-sounding words are written on Japanese products they seem to sell better on the home market. While many of the new words dreamt up by advertising agencies are unexceptionable, though a little odd when seen or heard by native English speakers, for example Sony's 'Walkman' cassette players, closely followed by 'Diskman' (portable compact disc) and 'Watchman' (portable TV), things can go awry sometimes, leading to interesting results:

Calpis	a make of sweet, fermented drink
Cedric	the most expensive of Nissan's car range
Creap	cream powder (for coffee)
Green piles	a lawn fertilizer
Little bugger	a make of model dump truck (possibly via the German 'Bagger' meaning excavator)
Mandom	a range of male toiletries
Rocket home pack	a make of water heater

lock (*on door*) jō
  it's locked kagi ga kakatte imas
  excuse me, I've locked myself out sumimasen, kagi o shimete shimaimashta

London Rondon

long nagai
  a long time nagai jikan

look: can I have a look? chotto mite mo ī des ka?
  I'm just looking, thanks ima, mite inu dake des, dōmo
  that looks good are wa, yosasō des
  I look forward to meeting you again mata o-ai suru no o tanoshimi ni shte imas

lorry torakku

lose (*key etc.*) nakusu /nakushimas/
  (*fight etc.*) makeru /makemas/
  I've lost my . . . . . . o nakushte shimaimashta
  I'm lost, can you help me? michi ni mayoimashta, taskete kudasaimasen ka?

lot: a lot of . . . . . . taksan no
  a lot zuibun
  a lot better zutto yoi
  not a lot (*small quantity*) taksan ja nakte
  (*not particularly*) betsu ni

love (*noun*) ai
  I love you (anata ga) dai-ski des
  The Japanese are less direct: this means literally 'I like you very much'.

lovely (*stay*) totemo tanoshī
  (*day*) totemo ī
  (*view*) subarashī

low hikui
  low prices hikui nedan

luck: good luck! gambatte kudasai!

luggage nimotsu
  my luggage nimotsu

lunch chūshoku, ranchi

LUNCH
Because most male Japanese city dwellers commute to work and don't come home before late at night, lunch tends to be relatively light. When working in the business district, **sararīman** (salaried workers) can take time off to visit one of the many small

restaurants in their vicinity, offering Japanese fare
(**wa-shoku**) or Western fare (**yō-shoku**) – *see* FOOD.
Lunch usually takes half an hour in a small restaurant, after which a coffee shop visit for twenty
minutes allows one to chat or relax before returning
to the office. Alternatively, they can consume a
boxed lunch (**o-bentō**) which their wives have made,
or which is quickly delivered from a nearby shop.
Since most Japanese food is eaten cold, or at best
tepid, there is no problem of having to heat anything
except the ubiquitous green tea (**o-cha**). *See also*
DINNER.

M

machine kikai

mad (*crazy*) kichigai
(*angry*) okotta

mail (*noun: letters*) yūbin
we'll mail it yūsō shimas

make tskuru /tskurimas/
our company make these kaisha ga kore o tskurimas

man otoko no hito
the man who ...... otoko no hito
the man who came yesterday kinō kita otoko no hito
the man whom we met yesterday kinō atta otoko no hito
Note that if no particular contrast with 'woman' is intended, then just **hito** will do:
>   **the man whom we met yesterday**
>   kinō atta hito

management: our management (*people*) (watakshi-tachi no) kei-ei
your management (anata no) kei-ei

manager (*of restaurant, hotel etc.*) shihai-nin
(*of business*) sekinin-sha

managing director torishimari yaku shachō

manners manā
good manners yoi manā
bad manners warui manā
See EMBARRASSMENT

many taksan (no)
there are not many taxis takshī wa amari ōku nai des

map chizu
I'd like a map of ...... no chizu ga hoshī des

March san-gatsu

market (*local market*) ichi-ba
(*for business*) shijō

MARRIAGE
In Japan almost everyone gets married, and there is strong pressure to conform. This is mainly based on

lingering Confucian ethics, where the continuation of the family line is of great importance, and where it is considered selfish to stay single. Match-makers (**nakōdo-san**), both amateur and professional, see to it that one can find the 'right' partner in an arranged marriage (**miai-kekkon**), but more and more young Japanese find partners for themselves these days. Their 'love marriage' is called **ren-ai kekkon**. Thus, be prepared to answer well-meaning and innocent questions such as:

> **nan-sai des ka?**
> how old are you?

to which you could reply:

> **san-jū go-sai des**
> I'm thirty-five

or:

> **kekkon shte imas ka?**
> are you married?

to which you can reply:

> **hai, kekkon shte imas**
> yes, I am

or:

> **īe, kekkon shte imasen**
> no, I'm not

or:

> **īe, mada des**
> no, not yet

The last three replies can be enlarged by 'fortunately' (**kō-un ni mo**) or 'unfortunately' (**zannen-nagara**), depending on your mood, for example:

> **zannen-nagara kekkon shte imasen**
> unfortunately I'm not married

married kekkon shta
I'm married kekkon shte imas

marvellous subarashī

MASCULINE FORMS *see* FEMININE FORMS

massage massāji

mat tatami

matches matchi

matter: it doesn't matter daijōbu des

mattress mattores

MATTRESSES

The term **mattores** refers to a Western-style bed, which takes up a lot of space and cannot be moved away in the daytime. Thus, most Japanese sleep on quilted bedding, called **futon**, which is spread on the floor at night. At bedtime the door of a large cupboard is slid open and the bedding taken out, having been stored there during the day. In theory, one **tatami** mat can accommodate one sleeper, so even a tiny room can sleep four persons, depending on the number of **futon** one has. Naturally, everyone has to go to bed at the same time, and sleeping late is impossible – in the daytime the room is used for other purposes. Furthermore, since they tend to get damp, **futon** have to be aired regularly and folded and stored in the cupboard. Western beds with mattresses, taking up a very large amount of space and restricting the use of the room, are luxury items for wealthy people, or for honeymoon couples in fancy hotels. This is one reason why Westerners find Japanese hotels so expensive – if they were content with simple **futon** on **tatami** mats in tiny rooms, prices would not be so high. Japanese inns or **ryokan** naturally provide **futon**, but the costs are high because of room size, additional meals and personnel costs.

maximum (*noun*) saidai

May go-gatsu

MAY

There are three possible uses here. The first one suggests the possibility of something happening and is formed simply by adding **kamo shiremasen** to the plain present form of the verb (*see* VERBS):

> **I may be late**
> okureru kamo shiremasen

> **I may go**
> iku kamo shiremasen

The second asks permission to do something and is formed by adding **mo ī des ka?** to the participle of a verb (*see* VERBS):

> **may I come in?**
> haitte mo ī des ka?

> **may I open the window?**
> mado o akete mo ī des ka?

The last type is a request for something and therefore requires a verb of receiving, such as **itadakemas ka?** or **moraemas ka?** (remember that the latter is less polite than the former). Alternatively, . . . **o o-negai shimas** could be used (*see* CAN):

> **may I have an orange juice?**
> orenji jūsu itadakemas ka?

maybe tabun

me watakshi
it's me watakshi des
that's for me sore wa watakshi ni des
See PERSONAL PRONOUNS

meal shokuji
that was an excellent meal sore wa, subarashī shokuji deshta
See EATING HABITS

mean: what does this sign mean? kono kigō wa dō iu imi des ka?

meat niku

medicine kusuri

meet: pleased to meet you o-ai dekite ureshī des
have you met the chairman? kaichō ni atta koto ga arimas ka?

meeting kaigi
shall we arrange another meeting? betsu no kaigi o shimashō ka?

MEETING PEOPLE
After the initial greetings (*see* HOW DO YOU DO?) it may be a good idea to engage in small talk somewhat longer than in your home country before coming to the point, assuming you do have some statement or request to make. If you are trying to speak in Japanese, you will invariably be lauded for your brilliant ability – *see* GUESTS.

Such small talk should ideally involve non-contentious things, such as the weather. While praising Japan in general, praising Japanese personally to their face (for example something they do, or wear etc.) will make them feel uncomfortable, since they are then forced to deprecate it. Don't admire some item too much in somebody's room or house – they might feel obliged to give it to you as a present!

mention: don't mention it dō itashimashte

menu menyū
the menu, please menyū o o-negai shimas
See FOOD

message dengon
can I leave a message? dengon o o-negai shte mo ī des ka?
can I leave a message for . . . ? . . . ni dengon o o-negai shte mo ī des ka?

metre mētoru

middle: in the middle of town machi no chūshin de
the middle of next month rai-getsu no nakagoro

midnight yo-naka

mile mairu

milk miruku

mine (*possessive pronoun*) watakshi no

mineral water (*carbonated*) tansan-sui
(*still*) mineraru uōtā

minimum (*noun*) saitei
with minimum expense saitei no hiyō de

minute fun
one minute ippun
two minutes nifun
five minutes gofun
ten minutes juppun
just a minute chotto

mirror kagami

Miss . . . . . . -san
Miss! (*to waitress etc.*) chotto!
See ADDRESSING PEOPLE
A polite way to call a waitress is to say 'excuse me' (**sumimasen!**), which is often abbreviated in such cases to **suimasen!**.

mistake machigai

MISTAKES
With the best will in the world, Westerners do make many mistakes which may offend those Japanese who have little knowledge of Western customs – *see* EMBARRASSMENT. And even those Japanese who have been abroad and who have rubbed shoulders with Westerners might feel offended at behaviour which

they would condone outside Japan but not inside their country.

In a society which is as different concerning basic views on human nature, and as intent on preserving surface harmony as Japan is, Westerners cannot help becoming the proverbial bull in the china shop on occasion, especially since they are, because of their size and colour, so eminently visible. Two factors add to the problem: on the surface Japan may look so Western that rich, casual visitors forget sometimes that they ever left home; and secondly, Japanese are rarely willing to point out the foreigner's mistakes, which could, if done tactfully, have prevented many unpleasant misunderstandings from developing.

Reading too many instructions about 'proper' behaviour can, naturally, inhibit one's actions to such an extent that nothing in this fascinating country will afford pleasure any more. However, as long as one's basic attitude is one of accepting the Japanese and their culture as they are on a basis of mutuality, and equality of respect and consideration, it should be possible to enjoy interacting with them.

What Japanese tend to credit is a foreigner's attempts to understand them – never mind if one in the end does not succeed. It is thus important to show that one is willing to learn and to be instructed. Sometimes this 'innocent ignorance' can be the best strategy, since attempts to conform all the time may lead to such tension that rapport becomes impossible.

modern gendai (no)
  modern Japan gendai no Nihon

Monday getsu-yōbi

money o-kane   お金

MONEY

Money in Japan (the Yen being the only unit) is often treated very discreetly. A tremendous amount of cash changes hands in Japan, suitably concealed in envelopes. If you are given an envelope with cash for some services rendered, you may be asked to sign a receipt. It may look a little tactless if you open the envelope and count the notes. In Japan, being short-changed is a very rare occurrence. However, if finally you do find less money in the envelope than you signed for, remember that sometimes 10 per cent is deducted at source for income tax purposes.

Money is rarely handed over directly. In shops it tends to be presented to you on a plastic dish. Again, it is hardly necessary to count it. Neither is tipping expected in restaurants etc., so nobody will watch you from the sidelines with bated breath, hoping for plenty to remain on the table.

At first the problem of having to deal in thousands of Yen (called **en** in Japanese) may be a bit unsettling, unless you arrived directly from Italy or Korea, where large denominations are also in daily use. A conversion table, based on the latest exchange rate between pounds or dollars and Yen, may make it easier to get your bearings. However, since there is no bargaining in Japan (except in the discount area for electronic goods in Tokyo, called Akihabara), all prices are fixed and you can, if unsure of how much you owe, just hand over money and request that the proper amount be deducted.

Some basic words and phrases:

money	o-kane
Yen	en
pound sterling	pondo
US dollars	doru
coin	kōka
banknote	satsu
ten Yen (coin)	jū-en (dama)
100 Yen (coin)	hyaku-en (dama)
1,000 Yen (note)	sen-en (satsu)
10,000 Yen (note)	ichiman-en (satsu)
small change	ko-zeni

how much is this?
kore wa ikura des ka?

it is 2,000 Yen
kore wa ni-sen-en des

this is free
kore wa sābis des
[*literally: this is service*]

I don't want this
kore wa kekkō des
[*literally: this is enough*]

could you change this into Yen for me?
kore o en ni kaete itadakemas ka?

could you give me some smaller change for this?
kore o ko-zeni ni kaete itadakemas ka?

month tsuki
    at the beginning of a month tsuki no hajime

before the end of the month getsumatsu mae ni
in a month's time hito-tsuki de

MONTHS

The months are named in a very simple fashion –
from 'first month' (January) to 'twelfth month'
(December):

January	ichi-gatsu
February	ni-gatsu
March	san-gatsu
April	shi-gatsu
May	go-gatsu
June	roku-gatsu
July	shichi-gatsu
August	hachi-gatsu
September	ku-gatsu
October	jū-gatsu
November	jū-ichi-gatsu
December	jū-ni-gatsu

Note also the method of counting months:

one month	ik-kagetsu
two months	ni-kagetsu
three months	san-kagetsu
six months	rok-kagetsu

Some useful phrases are:

in January
ichi-gatsu ni

at the end of February
ni-gatsu no owari

in the middle of March
san-gatsu no naka-goro

at the beginning of June
roku-gatsu no hajime

next month
rai-getsu

last month
sen-getsu

in three months from now
ima kara san-kagetsu ato ni

It is also worth noting that months in Japan are
frequently split up into ten-day periods:

1st – 10th	jōjun
11th – 20th	chūjun
21st – end	gejun

For example:

go-gatsu no jōjun
the first ten days of May

moon tsuki

moon-viewing tsuki-mi
As in China, the full moon of September (the harvest moon) is thought to be the most beautiful and is an occasion for thanksgiving and having a party.

more motto
no more thanks mō kekko des
could I have some more? mō skoshi itadaite mo ī des ka?
See COMPARISON OF ADJECTIVES

morning (*from 6 to 9 a.m.*) asa
(*before noon*) gozen
in the morning gozen ni
all morning gozenchū
tomorrow morning ashta no asa
this morning kesa
good morning o-hayō (gozaimas)

mosquito net kaya

most (*very*) ichiban
most interesting ichiban omoshiroi
most of them hotondo zembu

mother (*one's own mother*) haha
(*somebody else's mother*) okā-san

motor mōtā

motorcycle ōtobai

mountain yama

moustache kuchi-hige

mouth kuchi

Mr . . . . . . -san
See ADDRESSING PEOPLE

Mrs . . . . . . -san
See ADDRESSING PEOPLE

much: much bigger zutto ōkī
much faster zutto hayaku
there's not much left amari nokotte imasen

music ongaku

must

Although 'must' is a positive verb in English, its Japanese equivalent is negative and implies something like 'it won't do if I don't . . .' (i.e. 'I must').

To form this negative concept remove the final **-i** from a plain negative present verb (*see* NEGATIVES) and replace it with **-kereba narimasen**. For example:

tabenai [not eat]

I must eat
tabenakereba narimasen

nomanai [not drink]

I must drink
nomanakereba narimasen

ikanai [not go]

I must go
ikanakereba narimasen

If you just want to say 'I must' you could always use:

hitsuyō des
it's necessary, I must

my watakshi no
See POSSESSIVE ADJECTIVES

N

nail clippers tsume-kiri

nail scissors tsume-yō no hasami

name namae
   my name is ... namae wa ... des
   what's your name? o-namae wa nan des ka?
   what's his name? kare no namae wa nan des ka?
   what's her name? kanojo no namae wa nan des ka?
   what's the name of the hotel? hoteru no namae wa nan des ka?
   See ADDRESSING PEOPLE, CHRISTIAN NAMES

name card meishi
   See BUSINESS CARDS

napkin napkin

NAPKINS
When eating Western food, napkins are sometimes provided. For Japanese fare, the hand towels (**o-shibori**), discussed under EATING HABITS, can be used to wipe one's mouth or fingers during and after the meal. Since the **o-shibori** is damp, it is usually neatly folded after its initial use of wiping the hands, and placed next to a plate, either on a special dish or basket, or onto its plastic wrapping.

nationality kokseki

natural (*flavour, taste*) shizen (no)

near chikai
   is it near here? sore wa koko ni chikai des ka?
   is it near Sapporo? sore wa Sapporo ni chikai des ka?
   do you stop near ... ? ... no chikaku ni tomarimas ka?
   the nearest ... ichiban chikai ...
   where is the nearest ... ? ichiban chikai ... wa doko des ka?

necessary hitsuyō (na)

neck kubi

need: I need ...... ga irimas
   do you need ... ? ... ga irimas ka?
   See MUST

needle hari
    needle and thread hari to ito

NEGATIVES

Japanese has no single equivalent to the English word 'not'. Indeed, the Japanese negative has a verb form all of its own (which is why separate positive/negative listings are given under VERBS).

The polite negative causes no problems: simply change **-mas** to **-masen** and **-mashta** to **-masen deshta**:

> **sake wa nomimasen**
> I don't drink sake

> **nani mo tabete imasen**
> I'm not eating anything

> **Tōkyō ni wa ikimashta ga, Kyōto ni wa ikimasen deshta**
> I went to Tōkyō but I didn't go to Kyōto

The plain negative is somewhat more complicated. For Type 1 verbs, add **-nai** (present) or **-nakatta** (past) to the basic stem (*see* VERBS, Pattern A):

> **sushi wa tabenai**
> I don't eat sushi

> **sono eiga wa minakatta**
> I didn't see that film

For Type 2 verbs, change the final **-u** of the plain present to **-anai** (present negative) or **-anakatta** (past negative):

> **manga wa yomanai**
> I don't read comics

> **sake wa nomanakatta**
> I didn't drink sake

Note that in the case of the plain present form that ends in a vowel plus **u** (e.g. **arau**, **iu** etc.) a **w** is inserted before the negative suffix:

> **nani mo iwanai**
> he won't say anything

> **nani mo arawanakatta**
> I didn't wash anything

There are a small number of irregular plain negatives:

	present	*past*	
kuru	konai	konakatta	didn't come
suru	shinai	shinakatta	didn't do
aru	nai	nakatta	wasn't
da	de wā nai	de wā nakatta	wasn't

de wā often becomes **ja** (e.g. **ja nai** – it isn't)

For the problems in answering negative questions, *see* QUESTIONS.

negotiations kōshō

neither: which one? – neither dochira demo arimasen
  neither of them came dochira mo kimasen deshta
  he isn't going – neither am I kare wa ikimasen –
  watashi mo ikimasen

As you can see, the negative content of the word 'neither' must be conveyed in Japanese through a negative verb. The last example means, literally, 'I also am not going'.

nervous shinkei-shitsu (na)

net price seika

never

You use the word **kesshte** together with a negative verb:

> **I never go there**
> soko e wa kesshte ikimasen

> **we never go back on our word**
> yaksoku o yaburu yō na koto wa kesshte shimasen

If the 'never' appears in a 'have never done' type of sentence, use the plain past form followed by **koto ga arimasen**:

> **I have never been to Kyōto**
> Kyōto e itta koto ga arimasen

> **I have never seen one**
> mita koto ga arimasen

Note also the word **kamaimasen**, which means 'never mind'.

new atarashī

New Year shinnen
  Happy New Year! shinnen omedetō gozaimas!
  New Year's Day ganjitsu
  New Year's Eve ōmisoka

NEW YEAR

More than in most other countries, New Year in Japan is a season of renewal. Ideally, all outstanding debts should have been paid by midnight on 31 December, the house cleaned, rubbish thrown out, one's hair set or cut etc. At midnight there is the visit to the local shrine to pray for good luck in the coming year. The bell tolls one hundred and eight times to signal the passing of the old year.

For up to three days most shops are closed, but the public transport system will be working normally. Greeting cards are delivered during the first week of January, important persons receiving many hundreds. This is the Japanese family festival par excellence. Reciprocal visits in traditional dress are popular, so the whole country seems to be on the move – *see* HOLIDAYS. Traditionally, too, every Japanese became one year older on 1 January – a kind of collective birthday. Since a baby, when born, was reckoned to be one year old when it emerged from the womb, someone born on, say, 31 December would be considered two years old a single day later! Some older Japanese still count their age this way – it is called **kazoe-doshi**.

New Zealand Nyū Jīrando

news (*on TV etc.*) nyūs
   is there any news? nani-ka renraku ga arimas ka?

newspaper shimbun   新聞
   English newspapers (*written in English*) Eiji shimbun
   (*from the United Kingdom*) Igirisu no shimbun

next tsugi (no)
   next week raishū
   next month rai-getsu
   next year rainen
   at the next bus stop tsugi no bas-tei de
   next to the hotel hoteru no tonari de

nice (*person, meal, day*) steki (na)
   that's very nice of you go-shinsetsu des

night yoru
   good night (*going to bed*) o-yasumi nasai
   (*leaving work*) o-saki ni

no īe [ee-ay]
   there's no toilet paper toiretto pēpā ga arimasen
   I have no . . . . . . o motte imasen

NO

Although 'no' is correctly translated into Japanese as **īe**, this is seldom used in polite conversation since it sounds too abrupt. Anyway, the majority of questions are phrased in such a way that one should be able to reply in the affirmative. Surface harmony is considered a cardinal virtue, no matter how one might feel privately about something. One should therefore phrase questions carefully, although in the case of factual statements one can of course use **ie**. Here are some examples:

> **are you an American?**
> Amerika-jin des ka?
> [*literally: America person are (question word)*]

> **no, I am British**
> īe, Igirisu-jin des
> [*literally: no, England person am*]

To give a negative reply, a Japanese often leaves out the last part of the sentence. If he/she cannot come tomorrow, the reply might be:

> **no, I can't come tomorrow**
> ashta wa dōmo . . .
> [*literally: tomorrow as-for somehow . . .*]

'A little bit' (**chotto**) can also be used in the same way:

> **ashta wa chotto . . .**
> [*literally: tomorrow as-for a little bit . . .*]

Alternatively:

> **ashta . . .**
> tomorrow . . .

is said with a hesitant tone of voice.

nobody

Use **dare mo** with a negative verb:

> **nobody is in the office**
> jimusho ni wa dare mo imasen

> **nobody went**
> dare mo ikimasen deshta

normal futsū (no)

north kita
in the north kita ni

nose hana

NOT

Japanese has no one word corresponding to 'not'. For more on this *see* NEGATIVES. Here are some examples:

not for me, thanks o-kamai naku
(*if refusing food*) mō ī des, dōmo
not Tuesday ka-yōbi de naku

he's not here (kare wa) koko ni imasen
I'm not Mr Brown, I'm . . . (watakshi wa) Buraun dewa naku, . . . des

notebook te-chō

nothing
Use **nani mo** with a negative verb:

> **there is nothing there**
> nani mo arimasen

> **there is nothing left**
> nani mo nokotte imasen

> **I know nothing about it**
> sono koto wa nani mo shirimasen

NOUNS

Japanese nouns do not generally have plural forms and they do not indicate gender. Thus, **bīru** can mean: 'a beer', 'the beer', 'beers', or 'the beers'. **Hito** can mean: 'a person', 'the person', 'persons' or 'the persons'.

The relation between a noun and the rest of the sentence is indicated by placing one or more particles after it, of which the most important ones are **ga, wa, ni** and **e** (*see* PARTICLES).

One interesting aspect of many nouns (including foreign loan words) is that they can be changed into verbs by just adding **suru** (to do) (dictionary form) or **shimas** (polite form). Thus, **spōtsu** is the Japanese word for 'sports', and **spōtsu suru** is the equivalent for 'playing sports'. Don't be too surprised if you sometimes see T-shirt inscriptions on the chests of young girls, boldly proclaiming (in Japanese-style English):

> Let's sports violently all day long!

The common Japanese mistake, when speaking English, of saying: 'He marriaged her' can be explained in the same way: 'Marriage' is **kekkon** and 'to marry' in Japanese is **kekkon suru**. Translated back into English, this logically becomes 'to marriage'.

For honorific forms of nouns *see* POLITENESS LEVELS.

November jū-ichi-gatsu

now ima

number (*mathematical*) kazu
   (*house, telephone, etc.*) bangō
   what number is it? namban des ka?

NUMBERS *see* COUNTING OBJECTS

O

October jū-gatsu

OF

No, a postpositional particle (*see* PARTICLES), is the nearest Japanese has to the English 'of':

what is the name of the company president?
kaichō no o-namae wa nan des ka?

Note that English offers two possibilities of word order – 'the name of the product', or 'the product's name'. Japanese, however, gives only one choice:

seihin no namae
[*literally: product of name*]

kore wa Noguchi-san no kamera des
this is Mr Noguchi's camera
[*literally: this (as for) Noguchi-Mr of camera is*]

Japanese **no** replaces both 'of' and 's', and the learner must be careful to get the words in the right order.

This same function of **no** produces the possessive adjectives; for example:

my key
watashi no kagi
[*literally: I of key*]

The word **no** can also be used to indicate the material out of which something is made:

ki no tēburu
a table made of wood

OFF

There is no simple Japanese word for 'off'; very often, the English meaning is conveyed through a Japanese verb:

it's off (*machine*)
kirete imas

switch it off, please (*light, TV*)
keshte kudasai

should I take my shoes off?
kutsu o nuganakereba narimasen ka?

I must be off now
mō o-itoma shinakereba ikemasen

When children leave for school in the morning, or the husband for work, a common farewell is:

itte kimas
I'm off

or, more politely, **itte mairimas**, both meaning literally, 'I'll go and come back'. The proper response for those remaining behind is:

itte-rasshai

for which the nearest English equivalent is perhaps 'have a nice day', though literally it just means 'go and come back'.

offer (*noun*) teikyō
  we can offer . . . . . . o teikyō shimas

office (*workplace*) jimusho

official (*noun*) yaku-in

often tabi-tabi

oil (*on food*) abura
  (*for engines*) oiru

OK ī des, ōkē

old (*person*) toshiyori (no)
  (*thing*) furui
  how old are you? o-ikutsu des ka?

old-fashioned furui jidai no

on (top of) . . . . . . no ue [ooh-eh]
  on the table tēburu no ue ni
  on Tuesday ka-yōbi ni
  is it on? (*machine etc.*) kikai wa ugoite imas ka?
  (*lamp*) tsuite imas ka?
  a book on Japan Nihon ni tsuite no hon

one: one person hitori
  the first one (*person*) saisho (no)
  (*thing*) saisho (no)

only dake

open: is it open aite imas ka?
  are they open tomorrow? ashta wa aite imas ka?
  when do you open? itsu akimas ka?
  can I open the window? mado o akete mo ī des ka?

operation (*in hospital*) shujutsu

operator (*telephone*) kōkan-shu

opinion iken
  in my opinion watakshi no iken dewa

opposite hantai (no)

or mata-wa

orange juice orenji jūsu

order (*in business*) chūmon
 thank you for your order chūmon o arigatō gozaimas

order number chūmon-bangō

organize: well organized yoku soshki sareta
 poorly organized amari soshki sarete inai

other hoka (no)
 the other one (*person, thing*) hoka no

our watakshi-tachi no
 See POSSESSIVE ADJECTIVES

ours watakshi-tachi no

out: they're out (*lights*) kiete imas [ke-eh-te]
 she's out (*of house etc.*) (kanojo wa) imasen
 it will be out next month (*new model etc.*) sore wa
 raigetsu deru deshō

over: it's over (*finished*) owatte imas
 over 40 yon-jū ijō
 over there (*near you*) soko ni
 (*away from you*) asoko ni

overcoat ōbā-kōto

overnight (*travel*) yakō
 to go by overnight train yakō de iku ikimas

overseas kaigai (no)

oversleep: I'm afraid I overslept sumimasen, nebō shte
 shimaimashta

owe: we owe you . . . watakshi-tachi wa anata ni . . . no
 kari ga arimas
 you owe us . . . anata wa watakshi-tachi ni . . . no kari
 ga arimas

own: my own . . . watakshi-jishin no . . .
 your own . . . anata-jishin no . . .
 on one's own hitori de

owner mochi-nushi

P

packet tsutsumi
  a packet of . . . . . . hito-hako

pain itami

palace kyūden

paper (*sheet*) kami
  (*newspaper*) shimbun
  a piece of paper kami ichimai

paper folding origami

pardon? (*please say it again*) mō ichi-do itte kudasai

parents (*one's own*) ryōshin
  (*someone else's*) go-ryōshin

park (*noun*) kōen

part (*noun*) bubun

PARTICLES
Those Japanese units of speech which show the relationships inside a sentence are very different from the basic English parts of speech. They do not precede, but *follow* the word in question, with the function which prepositions and conjunctions have in English. They are, therefore, also called postpositions. Here are some examples of some of the more common Japanese particles:

ga
This particle indicates that the word which precedes it is the subject, and that this subject is somewhat more important than the verb which follows it. In English this is achieved by tone of voice, for example:

    ***he* came by car** (and not somebody else)
    kare ga kuruma de kimashta
    [*literally: he (subject) car by came*]

    I'd like some *milk* (and not something else)
    miruku ga hoshī des
    [*literally: milk (subject) desirable is*]

wa
If **wa** is used instead of **ga** to follow a word, it still

indicates that this is the subject, but the emphasis is more on that which follows. Roughly translated into English, **wa** becomes 'as for . . .':

he came by *car* (and not by something else)
kare wa kuruma de kimashta
[*literally: he as-for car by came*]

The distinction between **ga** and **wa** is a subtle one, which eludes many foreign speakers of Japanese. The learner might find it useful, however, to bear the following in mind:

(a) **ga** is always used when the subject of the sentence is an interrogative pronoun:

who came?
dare ga kimashta ka?

which one is mine?
dore ga watashi no des ka?

(b) **wa** is very often appropriate when the verb is **des**:

that's very cheap
sore wa totemo yasui des

is that gentleman over there the company president?
asoko no kata wa shachō des ka?

o

This particle indicates that the word immediately before it is the direct object of the verb. For example:

I (or you, he, she, etc.) **bought a camera**
kamera o kaimashta
[*literally: camera (object) bought*]

Note that personal pronouns (I, he, she etc.) are often omitted in Japanese. If you want to stress the pronoun and say:

he (NOT I, she, they etc.) **bought a camera**

you would phrase it:

kare ga kamera o kaimashta
[*literally: he (subject) camera (object) bought*]

And if he bought a camera and you do want to insert 'he', but without overemphasizing it, you would phrase it:

kare wa kamera o kaimashta
[*literally: he as-for camera (object) bought*]

ka

This particle comes at the end of the sentence, attached to the verb, and indicates that the sentence has become a question (*see also* QUESTIONS):

is it cold?
samui des ka?
[*literally: cold is (question)*]

With **ka** at the end to indicate a question, the voice need not be raised, as in English.

ne

Also occurring at the end, this particle conveys the feeling of an exclamation, or 'isn't it?':

it's cold, isn't it?
samui des, ne?
[*literally: cold is, isn't it*]

she's English, isn't she?
kanojo wa Igirisu-jin des ne?
[*literally: she as-for English person is, isn't she*]

See also IT.

Further particles equivalent to prepositions, adverbs and conjunctions are:

no

For the main use of the particle **no** *see* OF.

No can also be used with pronouns of place (which in English we would refer to as adverbs):

asoko no yama
that mountain over there
[*literally: over-there's mountain*]

koko no wa
as for this one here
[*literally: here's as-for*]

to

This can correspond either to the English 'with' (indicating that A is accompanying B), or 'and' (*see also* AND):

I drank beer with Mr Suzuki
Suzuki-san to bīru o nomimashta
[*literally: Mr Suzuki with beer (object) drank*]

I bought beer and coffee
bīru to kōhī o kaimashta
[*literally: beer and coffee (object) bought*]

kara

This corresponds to the English 'from' (either in space or in time):

is it far from England?
Igirisu kara tōi des ka?
[*literally: England from far is (question)*]

from next month
rai-getsu kara
[*literally: next-month from*]

See also BECAUSE.

made

This is similar to 'until', 'as far as', or 'up to' either in space or in time:

are you going as far as the station?
eki made ikimas ka?
[*literally: station to going (question)*]

until next month
rai-getsu made
[*literally: next-month until*]

ni

This can usually be translated as 'to' or 'in':

there are many Japanese in London
Rondon ni wa Nihon-jin ga taksan imas
[*literally: London in Japan persons (subject) many are*]

I sent a letter to Japan
Nihon ni tegami o okurimashta
[*literally: Japan to letter (object) sent*]

It can also be used to translate time phrases using 'in', 'on' or 'at':

on Tuesday
kayōbi ni

in November
jū-ichi-gatsu ni

at 6 o'clock
roku-ji ni

e

This indicates motion. The English equivalent is 'in' or 'towards' or 'into':

I am going to Osaka tomorrow
ashta Ōsaka e ikimas
[*literally: tomorrow Osaka towards go*]

de

This mainly has the function of 'with' or 'by', as well as 'at' (location) in English:

I ate it with chopsticks
hashi de tabemashta
[*literally: chopsticks with ate*]

> **he was sitting at the bar**
> bā de suwatte imashta
> [*literally: bar at was sitting*]

See also IN

mo

Used on its own, **mo** can be translated as 'even', 'also' or 'too':

> **he came too**
> kare mo kimashta
> [*literally: he also came*]

If you want to say 'both . . . and . . . ' the combination '**. . . mo . . . mo**' is used:

> **I drank both beer and coffee**
> bīru mo kōhī mo nomimashta
> [*literally: beer both coffee and drank*]

However, used with a negative verb, it means 'neither . . . nor . . .':

> **I drank neither beer nor coffee**
> bīru mo kōhī mo nomimasen deshta
> [*literally: beer both coffee and not-drank*]

partner (*in business*) shigoto no nakama

part-payment bunkatsu-barai

party (*celebration*) pātī

PASSIVE VERBS

Japanese has a passive just as English does:

> **I was told to come straight away**
> sugu kuru yō ni iwaremashta

The verb itself is formed by dropping the **-nai** of the negative plain form (here **iwa-nai**) and adding **-reru** (politely **-remas**) to Type 2 verbs (*see* VERBS). For example:

iwareru	be told
yobareru	be called

Type 1 verbs add the ending **-rareru** (politely **-raremas**). For example:

taberareru	be eaten
mirareru	be seen

Note that the irregular verb **suru** (to do) becomes **sareru**. The agent of the action (if expressed at all) is usually followed by **ni**:

> **(kare wa) junsa ni taiho saremashta**
> he was arrested by the policeman

The Japanese passive can be used to express the fact that an action is regarded as undesirable or inconvenient. For example:

dareka ni saifu o nusumaremashta
somebody stole my wallet, my wallet has been stolen (by somebody)

This leads to constructions that would not be possible in English:

kyonen oksan ni shinaremashta
he lost his wife last year
[*literally: he was died on by his wife last year*]

hisho ni yameraremashta
my secretary just quit
[*literally: I was quit on by my secretary*]

The Japanese passive can also be used to convey a sense of politeness or respect (in which use it has no connection with the English passive at all):

mō taberaremashta ka?
have you already eaten?

myōnichi koraremas ka?
will you be coming tomorrow?

In this last sentence both **myōnichi** (a more formal word for 'tomorrow' than **ashta**) and the use of the passive form indicate politeness.

Finally note that the English passive phrase 'has (already) been x-ed' is translated not by a passive form at all but rather by the participle (*see* VERBS) plus **aru /arimas/**:

the bill has already been paid
o-kanjō wa mō haratte arimas

has the letter been sent?
tegami wa okutte arimas ka?

passport ryoken, paspōto パスポート

past: past the crossroads/hotel kōsaten/hoteru o sugite

PAST TENSE
Japanese has only two real tenses, a present and a past. Intricate aspects of when something happened exactly (or will happen) are not of great concern to the Japanese language.

The past tense is equivalent to the English past 'I drank' as well as the perfect 'I have drunk'. Unlike English, where the past form is often irregular – 'see/saw', 'go/went' etc. – the Japanese way to indicate the past in verbs is regular except for the verb **suru** (to do) and **kuru** (to come). Here are some examples (for their formation *see* VERBS, PLAIN FORMS, NEGATIVES):

English	*present plain*	*present polite*	*past plain*
to drink	**nomu**	**nomimas**	**nonda**
to eat	**taberu**	**tabemas**	**tabeta**
to come	**kuru**	**kimas**	**kita**
to do, to make	**suru**	**shimas**	**shita**

past polite	*past polite (negative)*
nomimashta	**nomimasen deshta**
tabemashta	**tabemasen deshta**
kimashta	**kimasen deshta**
shimashta	**shimasen deshta**

The past negative in the plain style is formed by adding **-nakatta** to the negative stem (*see* NEGATIVES), as is shown in the example below:

I drink tea (*plain*)	**o-cha o nomu**
I drink tea (*polite*)	**o-cha o nomimas**
I drank tea (*plain*)	**o-cha o nonda**
I drank tea (*polite*)	**o-cha o nomimashta**
I didn't drink tea (*plain*)	**o-cha o nomanakatta**
I didn't drink tea (*polite*)	**o-cha o nomimasen deshta**

Here are some examples of the past tense in Japanese:

I come to Tokyo once a year
nen ni ichi-do Tōkyō e kimas

I came to Tokyo last year
kyo-nen Tōkyō e kimashta

we are doing business with . . .
. . . to shigoto o shte imas

we have done a lot of business with . . .
. . . to taksan no shigoto o shimashta

I can't hear
kikoemasen

I couldn't hear
kikoemasen deshta

it doesn't work
ugokimasen

it didn't work
ugokimasen deshta

are you going to London?
Rondon e iku tsumori des ka?

have you been to London?
Rondon e itta koto ga arimas ka?

he's arriving tomorrow
(kare wa) asu tsukimas

he arrived very early this morning
(kare wa) kesa totemo hayaku tsukimashta

they are major customers of ours
(karera wa) watakshi-tachi no tokui-saki des

they were major customers of ours
(karera wa) watakshi-tachi no tokui-saki deshta

Note that the same verb form covers all persons and singular/plural.

Unlike English, Japanese adjectives also have past forms, which are constructed by adding **-katta** to their basic stem (*see also* ADJECTIVES):

	present	*past*
high	**taka-i**	**taka-katta**
delicious	**oishi-i**	**oishi-katta**

Since these are plain forms, they cannot be used without **des** except in casual conversation to family or close friends. In polite conversation, **des** is added:

the tea was delicious
o-cha wa oishi-katta des
[*literally: (honorific) tea as-for delicious-was (polite)*]

path ko-michi

pavement hodō

pay harau /haraimas/
can I pay now, please? ima haratte mo ī des ka?
I'll pay for this watakshi ga haraimas

PAYING

If you are invited out, and have accepted, there is no question of 'going Dutch'. If you are a short-term guest in Japan, and if your host has an expense account, you do not need to reciprocate exactly. However, at some stage an invitation to a place you are familiar with (like a Western restaurant) may be a good way to keep things balanced. Should you have left Japan, a coffee-table book with beautiful photos of your home area or Britain in general might be a nice way to say 'thank you!'

Japanese are puzzled or amused when they see a group of Westerners call for the bill at a restaurant, and then go on to calculate each one's share down to the last Yen. Japanese, on the other hand, might almost get into a fight to decide on the privilege of who should pay. If you are the host, it is a good idea to excuse yourself some time before the end of the session, ostensibly going to the toilet, but in reality to settle your bill well in advance (*see also* HOST).

payment shiharai

pen pen

pencil empitsu

people hito-bito
a lot of people taksan no hito

pepper koshō

per: per night ippaku
per day ichi-nichi

per cent pāsento
25 per cent ni-jū-go pāsento
a 10 per cent discount jup-pāsento no nebiki

PER CENT
The word **pāsento** is, of course, a loan word from English. However, there is also a native word, **wari**, which is effectively a unit word for 10 per cent. Thus, **ichi-wari** equals 10 per cent, **ni-wari** 20 per cent and so on.

There is also the word **waribiki**, a discount, **ichi-waribiki** being a 10 per cent discount, **ni-waribiki** being a 20 per cent discount and so on.

perfect (*adjective*) kanzen (na)

PERFECT TENSE *see* PAST TENSE

perfume kōsui

perhaps tabun

permit (*noun: entry permit etc.*) kyoka

person hito

PERSONAL PRONOUNS
Westerners tend to use personal pronouns far too much when speaking Japanese. Unlike English speakers, the Japanese do not always bother to express things which they think the listener will know already. Of course there are ways of specifying them, but in Japanese many more things are im-

plied, while they must be spelled out in English.
Thus, in English one must say 'I go', 'you go' etc.,
while in Japanese **ikimas** is quite sufficient when
expressed in context and can mean either of these as
well as 'he goes', 'we go' etc. It is due to this fact that
pronouns are given in brackets in the translations in
this book and are sometimes omitted altogether.

Finally, it should be remembered that, on the
whole, the pronouns do not show respect and should
be avoided, especially when addressing one's superiors. If it does become necessary to use a personal
pronoun, for example when emphasizing or clarify-
ing something, the following words can be used:

I, me	**watakshi**	(male informal speech: **boku**) (female speech: **atakshi, atashi**) (*see* FEMININE FORMS)
you (*singular*)	**anata** **kimi**	(informal speech, to a subordinate)
he, him	**kare**	
she, her	**kanojo**	
we, us	**watakshi-tachi**	
you (*plural*)	**anata-tachi** **kimi-tachi**	(informal speech, to subordinates)
they, them (*masculine*)	**karera**	
they, them (*feminine*)	**kanojo-tachi**	

Note that subject pronoun and object pronoun are
the same. It is the following particle that differenti-
ates them (*see* PARTICLES).

Care should also be taken not to address Japanese
by **anata**, the direct translation of 'you'. For example:

anata wa o-genki des ka?

would be considered a bit odd as a translation for
'are you well?'. Although this is not in itself an
impolite form, it is considered too direct. Alterna-
tives are:

1. Omitting the personal pronoun completely:

o-genki des ka?

2. Using the person's family name (e.g. Mr Katō) and **-san**:

Katō-san wa o-genki des ka?

3. **Sensei** (the one who is senior) in the case of professors, teachers, or very high-ranking persons:

Katō sensei wa o-genki des ka?

or simply:

sensei wa o-genki des ka?

4. Using the person's correct rank in an organization. For example, in the case of a Section Chief (**kachō**):

kachō-san wa o-genki des ka?

[*literally: Section Chief (honorific) as-for (honorific) vigour is (question)*]

petrol gasorin

petrol station gasorin stando

phonecard terefon-kādo

photograph shashin

picture (*painting, drawing*) e

piece hito-kire
  a piece of ...... hito-kire

pig buta

pillow makura

pin pin

pinball pachinko

pipe (*to smoke, for liquid*) paipu

place (*noun*) basho

PLACE NAMES
Since virtually all place names in Japan are written in Chinese characters, a meaning can almost always be ascribed to them. Here are ten of the best-known Japanese place names, with their literal meanings attached:

Nihon/Nippon (Japan)	source of the sun
Tōkyō	eastern capital
Kyōto	capital city
Ōsaka	great hill
Hiroshima	wide island
Nagasaki	long promontory
Yokohama	side beach
Nikkō	sunshine

| **Honshū** | main states |
| **Fuji-san** | abundant warrior mountain |

PLAIN FORMS

Plain forms are the shortest, most abrupt verb forms and are to be avoided as main verbs in polite speech. These are the forms usually listed in a dictionary, however (indeed, they are often referred to as 'dictionary forms'). In this book, they are the first form given for verb entries.

All plain present positive forms end in **-u** (except the plain form of **des** (be), which is **da**). There are eleven possible endings:

Type 1	**-iru**	e.g.	**miru**	(see)
	-eru	e.g.	**taberu**	(eat)
Type 2	**-mu**	e.g.	**nomu**	(drink)
	-bu	e.g.	**yobu**	(call)
	-nu	e.g.	**shinu**	(die)
	-gu	e.g.	**nugu**	(remove)
	-ku	e.g.	**kaku**	(write)
	-ru	e.g.	**uru**	(sell)
	-su	e.g.	**hanasu**	(speak)
	-tsu	e.g.	**matsu**	(wait)
(*vowel*)	**-au**	e.g.	**arau**	(wash)

The plain past form is made by changing the final **-e** of the participle (*see* Pattern B under VERBS) to **-a**:

tabeta	I ate
nonda	I drank
tegami o kaita	I wrote a letter

The plain 'let's . . .' form is made by changing the **-ru** of Type 1 verbs to **-yō** (e.g. **tabeyō**, let's eat) and the **-u** of Type 2 verbs to **-ō** (e.g. **ikō**, let's go, **kaō** let's buy it).

It will be seen that all the forms given here are positive. The negative plain forms are treated separately (*see* NEGATIVES). Here are some examples of familiar, non-polite language, such as might be used between family members or close friends:

jūsu o katta
I bought some juice

mō dekita ka?
have you finished?

eiga o mi ni ikō
let's go see a film

Remember that **suru** (do) and **kuru** (come) have irregular plain forms:

	SURU	**KURU**
past (positive)	shta	kita
'let's'	shiyō	koyō

The verb **des** is also irregular:

plain present	**da**
plain past	**datta**

The plain form of **deshō** is **darō** (*see* FUTURE TENSE).

plastic puraschikku

plate sara

platform hōmu　ホーム
which platform? dono hōmu?
is this the platform for . . .? kore wa . . . yuki no hōmu des ka?

pleasant kimochi no yoi

please: yes please hai, o-negai shimas
can you please . . . ? . . . kudasaimas ka?
please do dōzo
please eat! dōzo tabete kudasai
please drink! dōzo nonde kudasai

PLEASE

If you want to indicate that you want something, the magic words are **o-negai shimas** for 'please', and **dōmo** for 'thank you'. **Dōmo** is actually a most useful word, having no real meaning in itself, but simply intensifying what follows (or intensifying that sentiment which is prevalent at that time, but which is not expressed in words). It effectively means 'very' or 'quite' – literally: 'in every way'.

As you arrive, as you interact, as you leave – all the time you can bow slightly, and say **dōmo** with a smile.

Note that **dōzo** means 'please' only in the sense of 'please do it', 'please go ahead' etc., allowing someone else to do something. For example, pointing to a doorway and saying **dōzo** means that you are allowing someone to go through the door before you, pointing to food and saying **dōzo** means 'please help yourself', and so on.

plenty taksan
plenty of . . . taksan no . . .

PLURALS

Japanese does not distinguish between singular and plural. For more details *see* A, AN.

pocket poketto

point (*verb*) yubisasu /yubisashimas/
  (*noun*) ten
  please point to it sore o yubisashte kudasai
  two point five ni ten go
  that's a good point sore wa ī kangae des

POINTING

In Japan it is considered rude to point at a person with one's finger. Neither should you point to objects with your foot.

police keisatsu 警察

policeman o-mawari-san

polite teinei (na)

POLITENESS *see* EMBARRASSMENT, FORMALITY, GUESTS, MISTAKES, VERBS

POLITENESS LEVELS

Among the world's major languages, Japanese is very special in respect of its complex language forms indicating the humbling of oneself or one's group and the corresponding respect language used to address persons who are seen as hierarchically superior. While German and French operate on two levels of intimacy/respect (*du/Sie* in German and *tu/vous* in French) – while English has none – Japanese has many more.

Nor do Westerners humble themselves any more, except at the end of formal letters. While 'I remain, Sir, your obedient servant' has all but disappeared these days in English letters, corresponding phrases are still flourishing in Japan.

While we sometimes also show politeness by the use of special phrases such as 'would the gentleman over there kindly . . . ?', 'may I please have your kind attention', 'allow me to say this with all due respect', most of this is indicated by tone of voice, hesitancy pauses and deferential forcefulness when interrupting.

Apart from all of the above, Japanese also uses different verbs for such occasions, as well as honorific prefixes and suffixes, to name just a few. These are really untranslatable and sound silly in English, since we do not talk of:

o-denwa
(your) honourable telephone

go-shujin
(your) honourable husband

o-jī-san
(your) honourable grandfather honourable

or even more politely:

o-jī-sama

While it is easy to make fun of this aspect of Japanese, for example by using words and phrases straight from Gilbert and Sullivan's *Mikado*, it will become clear that we sound funny to Japanese as well, since our politeness levels are rarely exactly right for the occasion when we try to speak Japanese. Indeed, as Western experts on the Japanese language tend to admit, the correct use of Japanese politeness levels is *the* most difficult feat in trying to master the language: one tends to be either just a little too polite, or not polite enough. All the more so since politeness levels may fluctuate ever so subtly during a conversation to create greater feelings of intimacy or aloofness, seniority or equality.

For instance, honorifics are also to be used for certain *things* belonging to persons close to a person one is talking to respectfully, although the former might not even be present, for example:

my telephone
denwa

your telephone
o-denwa

your grandfather's telephone
o-jī-san no o-denwa

When using verbs, you are advised to stick to the polite **-mas** form. You might sound rather over-polite and distant on occasion – but you are unlikely to offend anyone. From this it will be clear that Japanese, who feel most comfortable in surroundings where hierarchy is being emphasized, hate back-slapping Westerners who want to get on first-name terms the moment they have been introduced.

Here are some polite forms that you may hear or use:

1. Nouns: use of the prefix **o-** and **go-** and the suffix **-san** or **-sama** for people:

my husband
shujin

your husband
go-shujin

my letter
tegami

your letter
o-tegami

However, in the case of some nouns the honorific has become so standardized that it has lost its meaning, and is thus always to be used, for example:

o-cha
Japanese tea

gohan
boiled rice

Honorifics are especially important when talking about the relatives of your partner or those of a third person whom you regard as superior to yourself.

	your own	*another person's*	
		polite	*very polite*
wife	kanai	ok-san	ok-sama
husband	danna	danna-san	danna-sama
father	chichi	otō-san	otō-sama
mother	haha	okā-san	okā-sama
son	musko	musko-san	go-shi-soku
daughter	musume	musume-san	o-jō-sama

In this regard addressing someone with the direct equivalent of 'you' (**anata**) sounds impolite and blunt and is best avoided. For more on this *see* PERSONAL PRONOUNS.

Likewise you would not use the equivalent of 'she' (**kanojo**) when, say, talking about someone's daughter. To ask if she is well you would say:

musume-san wa o-genki des ka?
[*literally: daughter (as-for) (honorific) vigour is?*]

If actually talking to someone's daughter in the father's presence, her family name and **-san** would be used.

2. Verbs. As has been said the **-mas** form is a polite form of the verb. There are several more polite forms, however, as well as some important verbs which change their form completely according to politeness levels:

	speaking of oneself (humbling)	*speaking politely*	*speaking very politely*
to eat	**itadakimas**	**tabemas**	**meshiagarimas**
to be	**orimas**	**imas**	**irasshaimas**
to say	**mōshiagemas**	**īmas**	**osshaimas**
to see	**haiken shimas**	**mimas**	**goran ni narimas**

Another polite way of using verbs is to put them into the passive (*see* PASSIVE VERBS).

politics seiji

pork buta-niku

port (*for ships*) minato

porter (*in hotel: for bags*) bōi

POSSESSIVE ADJECTIVES
Possessives are formed by placing the particle **no** after the relevant pronoun (*see* PERSONAL PRONOUNS):

my	watakshi no
your	anata no
his	kare no
her	kanojo no

For example:

her name is Miss Tabata
kanojo no namae wa Tabata-san des
[*literally: her of name (as-for) Miss Tabata is*]

The point made in the entry under PERSONAL PRO-NOUNS about avoiding direct reference to a person due respect applies here too. Thus, speaking to a professor, one would say:

kore wa sensei no hon des ka?
is this your book, professor?

rather than:

anata no hon . . .

Similarly, 'the Section Chief's car' is referred to as:

buchō no kuruma
Section Chief's car

rather than:

kare no kuruma
his car

even if the English phrase is 'his car'.

possible kanō (na)
  is it possible to . . . ? . . . koto ga dekimas ka?
  as (soon) as possible dekiru dake (hayaku)

post office yūbin-kyoku 郵便局

postcard hagaki
  picture postcard ehagaki

POSTPOSITIONS *see* PARTICLES

potatoes jaga-imo

pound (*weight*) pondo
  (*sterling*) eikoku pondo

prefecture ken

prefer: which (of the two) do you prefer? dochira ga yoi
des ka?
  I prefer . . . . . . ga yoi des

present (*gift*) okurimono

PRESENT TENSE

Japanese has two tenses, present and past. In dictionaries verbs are usually listed in the plain present form. In this book, however, both the plain and polite present forms are given for convenience.

Remember that verbs stay the same regardless of person or number. For example:

      mainichi gohan o tabemas
can mean (I/you/he/she/we/they) eat(s) rice
            every day

The context in which the sentence is uttered will usually tell the listener who the subject is.

As well as the simple plain present form, there is a progressive form of the verb. The 'progressive form' is the form in 'he is coming, they are working' as opposed to 'he comes, they work'. In Japanese it is formed by adding **iru** (plain) or **imas** (polite) to the participle (*see* VERBS, Pattern B):

  nani o yatte iru? (*plain*)
  what are you doing?

  tegami o kaite imas (*polite*)
  I'm writing a letter

  ame ga futte imas (*polite*)
  it's raining

It should be noted, however, that this 'progressive' form is not completely identical to the English progressive. This becomes clear when we meet sentences like:

> **Amerika e itte imas**
> he has gone to America

> **hako ni haitte imas**
> it's in the box

What these sentences demonstrate is the way the Japanese progressive, unlike its English counterpart, can describe a state resulting from an action (i.e. 'he has gone to America and is therefore in America', or 'it has entered the box and is therefore in the box'). Such sentences as the following, then, must be treated with especial care:

> **inu wa shinde imas**

does not mean:

> the dog is dying

but: the dog is dead

On the whole, though, participle plus **iru/imas** will correspond to English progressives. Here are some more examples:

> **nani o shte imas ka?**
> what are you doing?

> **tomodachi o matte imas**
> I'm waiting for my friend

Finally, it should be noted that one verb in particular, **shiru** (to know), is always used as a progressive when positive:

> **shitte imas ka?** (*polite*)
> do you know?

> **shitte iru** (*plain*)
> I know

> **shitte imashta** (*polite*)
> I knew

See also VERBS, NEGATIVES, PLAIN FORMS

president (*of state*) dai-tōryō
(*of firm*) shachō

pretty kirei (na)

price nedan
that's our best price sore wa ichiban yasui nedan des

private kojin (no)
in private (*talk etc.*) naishō de

probably tabun

problem mondai
   we've had some problems ikura-ka mondai ga arimashta
   that's no problem! sore wa mondai ja arimasen!

product seihin

production manager seihin sekinin-sha

profit ri-eki

pronounce hatsuon suru /hatsuon shimas/
   how is it pronounced? sore wa dono yō ni hatsuon shimas ka?

PRONOUNS *see* PERSONAL PRONOUNS

PRONUNCIATION
Correct Japanese pronunciation need present no major problems to English speakers if it is remembered that the basic unit is the syllable, and not the letter. In theory, except for the consonant **n**, which may itself constitute a syllable, all syllables end in a vowel. Therefore, all foreign loan words are assigned vowels at the end. For example:

   fork   **fōku**
   knife **naifu**

On the whole, every syllable of each word is given equal stress. This is quite unlike English, where meaning can alter dramatically depending on stress alone:

I saw him!   I *saw* him!   I saw *him*!

Such differences are indicated in Japanese by changing the particles after subject and object (*see* PARTICLES).
   If you speak evenly and slowly, most Japanese should have no trouble understanding what you are trying to say. However, care must be taken to pronounce a vowel in the Italian or German way, i.e. keeping it as a single pure sound and not changing it to another vowel halfway through. Uninitiated English speakers tend to call the capital city of Japan **Tow-kyow**, and, even worse, the capital of ancient Japan **Key-ow-tow**. In all these cases, the **o** sound should stay constant, and not change from o to ow. The cities mentioned above are then written as **Tōkyō** and **Kyōto**, respectively.

In the example of **Kyōto** the first **o** is pronounced twice as long as the second one. This is indicated by a macron (ˉ) over the relevant vowel.

Pronouncing a word incorrectly may change its meaning completely. For example:

| timepiece, watch | **tokei** |
| statistics | **tōkei** |

Mixing these two up is not in itself serious, but it can be if one mentions the advisor of the high-ranking person one is talking to:

| advisor | **komon** |
| anus | **kōmon** |

Sometimes the letters **i** and **u** are not fully sounded (especially in the Tōkyō dialect, which is rather clipped, and which has strongly influenced standard Japanese pronunciation). In such cases, **-masu** is pronounced **-mas**, **-mashita** is pronounced **-mashta**, **desu** is pronounced **des**, **deshita** is pronounced **deshta**, etc. The clipped form has been used in all relevant examples in this book.

Some clipping also occurs with the **-ya**, **-yu** and **-yo** syllable, as was shown already in the example of Tōkyō and Kyōto. The combination **kyo** is not pronounced **ki-o** or **ke-o**, but **k'yo**, i.e. **k** and **y** sounds follow one another rapidly. Similarly, the **Kyū** of **Kyūshū** sounds like the 'cu' of an English word like 'cute'.

A change from single to double consonant in English rarely changes the word's meaning; for example if we write 'speling' instead of 'spelling' it is incorrect, but still intelligible. However, in Japanese the doubling of a consonant can alter the whole meaning, so care should be taken to pronounce each consonant separately, rather like in 'dru*m-ma*jor'. Japanese examples of change in meaning are:

| **coming** | kite |
| **postage stamp** | kitte (pronounced 'kit-te') |

| **hole** | ana |
| **such** | anna (pronounced 'an-na') |

To voice the Japanese **r** sound correctly is rather difficult at first, because it is a blending of the English *d*, *l* and *r* sounds. One way to practise is to pronounce **origami** (the art of folding paper) as 'oddi-gami', and **eri** (collar) as 'eddy'. Notice how the tip of your tongue hits the ridge behind your

teeth very briefly, dropping down immediately afterwards.

A pronunciation guide for consonants and vowels
used in Japanese is listed on page ix of this book.

publicity kōkoku

pull hiku /hikimas/ 引く

pure (*substance*) junsui (na)

push osu /oshimas/ 押す

Q

quality hinshitsu
    quality goods (*good quality*) yoi seihin

quality control hinshitsu kanri

quarter yombun no ichi

quarter of an hour jū-go-fun

QUESTIONS

Forming questions in Japanese is very simple – just add **ka?** to a statement:

> **atsui des**
> it's hot

> **atsui des ka?**
> is it hot?

> **Sumisu-san wa shachō ni aimashta**
> Mr Smith met the company president

> **Sumisu-san wa shachō ni aimashta ka?**
> did Mr Smith meet the company president?

Great care should be taken, however, when it comes to *negative* questions. It is not their formation which is difficult (again, just add **ka?**) but their correct interpretation. When we answer questions in English, we tend to use 'yes' with a positive verb and 'no' with a negative verb, regardless of the type of question.

In Japanese, on the other hand, the 'yes/no' response refers purely to the correctness of the assumption behind the question. In effect, this means that **hai** (which usually translates 'yes') and **īe** (usually translating 'no') are used in a way quite contrary to English:

> **aite imasen ka?**
> isn't it open?

> **hai, aite imasen**
> *no*, it isn't

> **īe, aite imas**
> *yes*, it is

In the first response the Japanese is saying 'yes, you are right in assuming it is not open'. In the second response the Japanese is saying 'no, you are not right in assuming it is not open'.

Note that this problem does not arise with *positive* questions:

aite imas ka?
is it open?

hai, aite imas
yes, it is open

ie, aite imasen
no, it isn't open

quick hayai

quickly hayaku
   as quickly as possible dekiru dake hayaku

quiet shizuka (na)

quite: quite a lot kanari taksan

quote (*noun: for job etc.*) mitsumori

R

radio rajio
  on the radio rajio de

rail: by rail densha de

rail pass teiki-ken

railway station eki 駅

rain (*noun*) ame
  it's raining ame des

raincoat reinkōto

rainy season tsuyu

rate of exchange kawase sōba 為替レート

razor (*electric*) denki kamisori
  (*wet*) kamisori

read yomu /yomimas/
  could you read it out for me? sore o yonde kudasaimas ka?

ready: are they ready? (*items*) dekite imas ka?
  are you ready? ī des ka?
  I'm not ready mada des

real hommono (no)
  a real pearl hommono no shinju
  is it the real thing? hommono des ka?

receipt uketori
  can I have a receipt? uketori o morae-mas ka?

receive (*goods etc.*) uketoru /uketorimas/

reception (*desk at hotel*) furonto
  (*ceremony*) kangeikai
  wedding reception shinkon hirōen

red akai

reduced price nebiki-ne

reference number sanshō bangō

registered mail kakitome yūbin
  by registered mail kakitome yūbin de

reliable: he's reliable (kare wa) shinrai dekimas

remember omoidas /omoidashimas/

rent (*verb: car etc.*) kariru /karimas/

repair shūri
   it needs repairing shūri ga hitsuyō des

repeat kurikaesu /kurikaeshimas/
   please repeat that sore o kurikaeshte kudasai

reply (*noun*) henji
   we look forward to your reply go-henji o o-machi
shimas

representative (*noun: of company*) dai-hyō-sha

reserve (*seat*) yoyaku suru /yoyaku shimas/
   can I reserve a seat? seki o yoyaku dekimas ka?

restaurant restoran *or* ryōriten
　レストラン　　料理店

RESTAURANTS

In the big Japanese cities there are many restaurants
specializing in the food of various countries. The
most frequent foreign-food restaurants are Chinese
ones, especially in Yokohama, followed by Korean-
style restaurants, where grilled meat dishes are
served, together with hot pickled Chinese cabbage
(**kimchi**). Since Japanese do not care much for hot
and spicy food, foreign food is usually served more
bland than in its home country.

While Western eating utensils can be provided, it
is best to practise how to use chopsticks (**o-hashi**)
before visiting Japanese restaurants. Japanese chopsticks of the wooden variety (**waribashi**), shorter than
Chinese ones, are broken apart before being used.

Choice of food in a restaurant is rarely a problem
because realistic wax models of the whole menu are
displayed at the entrance. You can then summon a
waiter or waitress (with sign language, if necessary)
and point to what you want. Since there is no
tipping, you will often be charged exactly what is
written next to the dish of your choice. However, in
traditional restaurants the price is sometimes written
in Chinese-derived figures and not in Arabic numerals. In such cases you can ask for the price to be
written down after saying:

   sore wa ikura des ka?
   how much is that?

   chotto, kaite kuremasen ka?
   could you please write it down?

Remember, however, that with the 1989 introduction of a so-called 'consumption tax', 3 per cent may be added to the given price.

Especially pleasant for Western children (and adults who have remained children at heart) is the custom of slurping when eating noodles – it makes them taste better. Try it!

Some words and phrases:

restaurant	**restoran**
Western-style cuisine	**seiyō ryōri**
Chinese-style cuisine	**chūka ryōri**
Korean-style cuisine	**kankoku ryōri**
Japanese-style cuisine	**Nihon ryōri**
Japanese haute cuisine	**kaiseki ryōri**
regional specialities	**kyōdo ryōri**
vegetarian cuisine	**shōjin ryōri**

teishoku
set meal with rice, soup, pickles and main dish

o-hiru no teishoku
set meal, lunchtime

higawari teishoku
set meal of the day

sashimi teishoku
set meal with raw fish as the main dish

tempura teishoku
set meal with deep-fried prawns as the main dish

tonkatsu teishoku
set meal with pork as the main dish

yakiniku teishoku
set meal with grilled meat as the main dish

See also FOOD

return kaeru /kaerimas/ (*see also* **go**)
  a return ticket to . . . . . . made no ōfku-kippu

rice (*uncooked*) kome
  (*cooked*) gohan
  (*when served Western-style*) rais

rice bowl chawan

rich (*person*) kanemochi (no)

right (*correct*) tadashī
  (*direction*) migi
  that's right sō des

all right (*I agree*) ī des
I'm all right, thanks (*not hurt etc.*) dai-jōbu des, dōmo
that's all right (*doesn't matter*) sore de ī des
on the right migi-gawa ni

rights (*to manufacture etc.*) kenri

river kawa

road michi

room heya   部屋
I'd like a room for two nights ni-haku de heya ga hoshī des
in my room watakshi no heya de

ROOMS

The most important rooms in a Japanese house are:

the guest room
kyaku-ma

the kitchen
daidokoro

the living-room
ima

the tatami room
tatami-beya (*used for sleeping*)

the bathroom
o-furo-ba (*never with a toilet*)

the toilet
toire

the entrance hallway
genkan

rubber (*material*) gomu
(*eraser*) keshi-gomu

rubbish (*waste*) gomi
(*poor-quality goods*) furyō-hin

rude burei (na)

RUDENESS

Westerners often comment on the Japanese switch in behaviour, from polite to rude and vice versa. Although on the whole Japanese are quite polite (or at least non-committal) towards strangers, they can be very rude towards low-prestige persons *inside* their own group, for example husbands towards wives, bosses towards women in their office etc.

S

sad (*person, news*) kanashī

safe (*not dangerous*) anzen (na)
  (*not in danger*) dai-jōbu

sake bottle tok-kuri

sake cup sakazuki

salad sarada

salary kyū-ryō

sale: for sale urimono no

sales director hanbai sekinin-sha, hanbai torishimariyaku

salesman hanbai-in

salt shio

same onaji
  the same again please onaji mono o mō hitotsu o-
  negai shimas

sample (*noun: of goods, of work*) mihon

sandwich sando-ittchi

Saturday do-yōbi

say iu /īmas/
  what did he say? (kare wa) nan to īmashta ka?
  he said ... (kare wa) ... to īmashta
  how do you say ... in Japanese? ... wa Nihongo de
  nan to īmas ka?
  how do you say it? (*pronounce*) dono yō ni īmas ka?

scarf skāfu

schedule yotei
  work is on schedule shigoto wa yotei-dōri des
  work is behind schedule shigoto wa okurete imas

school gakkō

scissors hasami

Scotland Skottorando

sea umi
  by sea (*travel*) kairo de
  (*send mail*) funabin de

seal: personal seal hanko

seat seki

seaweed kaisō

second (*adjective*) dai-ni no

second class (*travel*) ni-tō

second-hand chūko

secretary hisho
   my secretary watakshi no hisho
   his secretary kare no hisho

see miru /mimas/
   can I see it? mite mo ī des ka?
   have you seen my colleague? dōryō ni atta koto ga
   arimas ka?
   I saw him a few minutes ago ni-san-pun mae ni kare
   ni aimashta
   let's wait and see matte mimashō
   oh, I see ā, wakarimashta

sell uru /urimas/
   we sell . . . . . . o urimas

send okuru /okurimas/
   we'll send it out to you anata ni okurimas

September ku-gatsu

serious (*situation*) jūdai (na)
   this is very serious kore wa, totemo jūdai des

sex (*gender*) sei
   (*sexual activity*) sekksu

SEX

Owing to the fact that Japan's indigenous religion,
Shintō ('The Way of the Gods'), places great stress
on fertility and procreation, sex has always been
viewed as something positive, provided it finds its
outlet in the 'proper place'. This is in strong contrast
to Christianity, which regarded sexuality as a necessary evil – unfortunately indispensable for procreation, but otherwise distracting the true believer from
concentrating on the eternal life which is to come.

   From this it could be concluded that Japan is a
country of unbridled lust, but this is far from the
truth. On the surface (except for the amusement
districts in large cities) Japan actually resembles
Victorian Britain – couples are hardly ever seen
kissing in public, for instance. However, out of sight,
in love hotels, film theatres, massage parlours and a
host of other establishments catering directly for the

basic needs of a predominantly male clientèle, everything imaginable can be experienced in the realm of sexuality.

In Japan sex is regarded as a minor pleasure, to be enjoyed fully in its proper time and place, but only after having fulfilled one's more pressing obligations, especially towards workplace and family.

However, another paradox emerges when the Westerner accompanies Japanese businessmen to, say, a hostess bar: he will find that although the atmosphere is full of erotic innuendo, very little overt sexuality is actually shown there. Neither is very much going on between hostess and client after the bar closes. This is due to the fact that most of this banter is intended to impress on one's other male companions how important one is, being able to summon the services of such lovely women. From a Western viewpoint a lot of this sexual play has a distinctly infantile flavour. Naturally, this is a biased view, since, from the Japanese viewpoint, such behaviour is perfectly normal, and, by contrast, Westerners' attitudes can be regarded as 'uptight'.

Japanese females are therefore constrained not so much by feelings of 'sinfulness', but rather by 'impropriety'. While there is endless discussion of the most intimate sexual questions in magazines and comics for young girls, the readers must openly pretend to know nothing, and possess (or feign) virginity until their wedding day. After that, their major emotional tie is with their children (who ideally start emerging nine months after the marriage). The husband is mostly seen as a rather distant person, of major importance only for providing status and a regular income for the family. If he has a mistress or two in later life (once he can afford them), this is something a wife has to accept, rather like accepting that a little child must have a new toy. As long as this attachment doesn't lead to a full-blown love affair, ending in divorce and its attendant miseries, men's extramarital escapades (usually in the company of his fellow workers) are grudgingly condoned.

Western men should therefore be prepared to answer rather intimate questions concerning their love life once they start drinking with Japanese male acquaintances.

shake yusuru /yusurimas/
  shake hands akshu suru /akshu shimas/

SHAKING HANDS

Shaking hands is virtually unknown among Japanese, who prefer bowing – despite having so many other Western imports. However, when meeting Westerners, a hand is frequently offered and a limp handshake, often accompanied by a slight bow, may result. Japanese are rarely taught that Westerners tend to judge a person's character by his firm grip and his steady eye contact when shaking hands. In fact, such behaviour is viewed by Japanese as positively threatening, and should therefore be underplayed. In both instances the Japanese are often sadly deficient, which leads some Westerners to conclude that they are weak and shifty characters. Beware of such a false generalization. And for your own part, relax your vice-like grip and remember that Japanese dislike the steady gaze. *See also* EYE CONTACT

shame: that's a shame zannen des

SHAME

It is all too easy to classify Japan as a 'shame culture', where one does or doesn't do things because others are always watching or listening, as opposed to the Western 'guilt culture', where some all-seeing god is (or was) always lurking above the clouds. For one thing, Japanese do have many guilt feelings – not towards any god or gods, perhaps, but often towards their silently suffering mothers.

On the other hand there is little doubt that 'shame' is a powerful motivating force in Japan. Little children are brought up with the admonition that others will laugh at them if they make mistakes. Keeping the proper 'face' – one's own, as well as that of one's family, one's work group, and, in the international sphere, one's country – is of great importance. This is aided inside Japan by the elaborate speech conventions in which one praises one's opposite while humbling oneself (*see* POLITENESS LEVELS).

Feeling shame implies, of course, that one is constantly surrounded by persons who matter. Therefore, in large cities and anonymous crowds this feeling of shame can disappear. Outside Japan, too, behaviour is often strongly at odds with polite behaviour shown inside the country. The Japanese proverb, **Tabi no haji wa kakisute** ('Scratch off shame when you are away on a trip') highlights this.

Complaints are regularly received from less affluent Asian countries, where Japanese men arrive in large groups to take over the night spots and monopolize the women.

To Westerners, Japanese therefore often seem to be thinking less in terms of abstract ethical principles and more in terms of concrete situations; they conclude from this that they are weak and unprincipled. On the other hand, Japanese often tend to regard Western behaviour as being shamelessly self-righteous and lacking in human feelings.

shampoo (*noun*) shampū

sharp (*blade*) surudoi
  (*taste*) pirit-to

shave (*verb*) soru /sorimas/

shaver hige-sori

shaving soap hige-sori yō-sekken

she kanojo
  See HE

ship fune
  by ship (*mail*) funabin de
  by ship (*transportation*) fune de

shipping company (*for freight*) kai-un-gaisha

shirt waishatsu

shoe kutsu

SHOES
An important custom is the invariable removal of shoes on entering a Japanese private house. This is a custom often copied by Westerners returning to their own country, since it keeps the home uncontaminated by dirt from the streets. Naturally, walking around in one's best suit but with slippers takes some getting used to. Take care never to have holes in your socks! Furthermore, such slippers should be taken off when stepping onto **tatami** mats. Finally, special slippers are provided for the toilet – take care to change back to your regular slippers on leaving the **o-tearai** (literally: 'honourable hand-washing (place)').

shop (*noun*) mise

short mijikai
  (*person*) se ga hikui

(*time*) skoshi

shoulder kata

show: can you show me? watakshi ni misete kuremas ka?
can you show me how it works? tsukai-kata o misete kuremas ka?

shower shawā
I'd like to take a shower shawā o abitai des

shrine jinja

shut (*transitive verb*) shimeru /shimemas/
(*intransitive verb*) shimaru /shimarimas/
it's shut shimatte imas

sick (*ill*) byōki
I'm feeling sick (*like vomiting*) kimochi ga warui des

side (*of box etc.*) waki
on the left-hand side hidari-gawa ni

sights: the sights of . . . . . . no kembutsu

sign (*by signature, Western-style*) sain suru
(*by name seal*) hanko o osu
please sign here (*Westerners*) koko ni sain shite kudasai
(*Japanese*) hanko o koko e oshite kudasai
where do I sign? doko ni sain suru no des ka?

signature (*Western*) sain
(*Japanese*) hanko

silk kinu

silver gin

similar: it's similar nite imas
it's similar but not the same nite imas ga, onaji de wa arimasen

since: since our last meeting mae no kaigi irai
since last year kyonen irai

sing utau /utaemas/

single: I'm single dokshin des

single room hitori-beya

single ticket katamichi no kippu

sir (*polite*) -san
(*very polite*) -sama
See ADDRESSING PEOPLE

sister (*general*) shimai
(*older, talking about one's own*) ane

(*older, someone else's*) o-nēsan
(*younger, talking about one's own*) imōto
(*younger, someone else's*) imōto-san
See BROTHER

sit suwaru /suwarimas/
can I sit here? koko ni suwatte mo ī des ka?
please sit down dōzo osuwari kudasai

SITTING

In formal situations you are likely to be the guest of honour. In all cases watch your host closely and take the seat assigned to you. In a traditional Japanese room, the seat of honour is the **kami-za** (literally: the upper place) with the back to the **tokonoma** (alcove) in which flower arrangements are placed and where a beautiful scroll is hung. Seats of successively lower rank are closer to the door – the **shimo-za** (literally: low place) being nearest the door. In ancient times, the 'upper place' was also the safest one, for one's enemies would first have to get past one's retainers after charging through the door, while the alcove side was protected and fortified at the back by the thick pillar which held up the house.

size (*of clothing*) ōkisa

skin hada

skirt skāto

sky sora

sleep (*verb*) nemuru /nemurimas/
I need some sleep suimin ga hitsuyō des
did you sleep well? yoku nemure-mashta ka?

sliding door (*with thick paper covering*) fusuma
(*with thin paper covering*) shōji

slippers surip-pa

slow osoi
very slowly totemo osoku

small chīsai
(*room, house*) semai

You will frequently find 'small' translated by a prefix such as **ko-** or **shō-**. For example:

kobotoke	a small Buddha image
kozutsumi	a small package
shōni	a small child
shōryō	a small quantity

smell (*noun*) nioi

smile (*noun*) hoho-emi

SMILES *see* FACIAL EXPRESSIONS

smoke: do you smoke? (*offering cigarette*) tabako o
suimas ka?
  may I smoke? tabako o sutte mo ī des ka?

SMOKING

While Japanese women rarely smoke in public,
males tend to smoke like chimneys, especially in
long-distance trains and aircraft. Permission to
smoke is rarely requested – and, among polite
Japanese, once asked, who can refuse? A recent
petition to have more than just the very front end of
the 'bullet train' reserved for non-smoking has
unfortunately failed.

However, there is a total ban on smoking in
suburban trains (and buses), which keeps the station
master and his staff busy sweeping up discarded
butts from the platform almost all day long. They
get a respite during the two main rush hours, when
there is a ban on smoking on platforms as well.

There is aggressive advertising, especially by
American cigarette companies, which have recently
been allowed to sell in Japan after the government's
tobacco monopoly was revoked – one rather sad
result of Japan's market liberalization policy.

snow (*noun*) yuki

so (*very*) taihen
  it's so warm taihen atatakai des

soap sekken

socks kutsushta

soft drink softo dorinku

software softo u-eā

sole rights doksen kenri

some
  The word 'some' may often be omitted in translation:

  I need some stamps
  kitte ga irimas
  I'd like some tea
  o-cha ga hoshī des

When it is needed the word **ikutska** can be used, with **no** added if used before a noun:

> **some of them are cheap**
> ikutska wa yasui des
>
> **some of the company's products**
> kaisha no seihin no ikutska
>
> **some of the wooden dolls**
> ikutska no kokeshi

In the construction 'some . . . others . . .' the word **aru** can be used:

> **some people can, some can't**
> aru hito wa dekimas ga aru hito wa dekimasen

somebody dare-ka

something nani-ka

sometimes toki-doki

somewhere doko-ka de

son musko

soon sugu ni
  as soon as possible dekiru dake hayaku
  we'll be back soon sugu modorimas

sorry sumimasen
  I'm very sorry (*apology*) sumimasen

SORRY

As is to be expected, Japanese have a wealth of phrases to indicate that they are sorry for something which has happened inside their sphere of responsibility.

However, there is an interesting paradox – apologies are really only used towards those with whom one has established some prior contact. Complete outsiders, such as passengers on a crowded subway train whom one collides with, are not asked for their pardon at all. This is not so much because of disdain for unknown persons, but rather that they don't really exist unless introduced. Nor do Japanese tend to get involved in public if somebody falls down or is in obvious need of help, unless they know that person.

This situation changes drastically when one's opposite has become a 'significant other'. One Western lady used this to good effect: before trying to board a train during rush hours, she would introduce herself to some tough-looking male on the platform by innocently asking for directions, etc.

When the crowded train arrived, her new-found acquaintance then felt under obligation to assist her inside.

Indeed, compared with Westerners, Japanese seem to be forever apologizing to their friends and acquaintances, even when there seems to be no discernible reason. Apologizing for a 'trifling gift' (when it seems quite splendid) or for 'having nothing in the house' when being led to a sumptuous banquet are just two instances when Westerners feel ill-at-ease or amused. Should they apologize as well under similar circumstances?

Here some middle position needs to be taken. Apologizing as much as Japanese are wont to do will look ridiculous. Anyway, English is rather clumsy and curt when it comes to this – how many other words besides 'sorry!' do we possess? However, one should obviously be somewhat more apologetic than in one's home country.

It should be kept in mind that in Japan gratitude is closely related to apologizing for having caused trouble to other persons.

The major phrases for saying 'sorry!' are:

mōshiwake arimasen-ga . . .
I'm very sorry to trouble you, but. . .
used when approaching somebody.

sumimasen
[*literally: (the obligation) never ends*]
is not used only to indicate apologies, but can also mean a simple 'thank you'. Thus, on receiving a gift, one often says **sumimasen** instead of **arigatō gozaimas**, as the former is considered more polite. To be quite accurate, **sumimasen** should be used when one did not have cause to expect some favour. In such a case simple thanks are not enough – one should apologize for having caused trouble.

o-jama shimashta
[*literally: I'm sorry I disturbed you*]
While Westerners express their gratitude for a nice time on leaving the hosts, Japanese will apologize for taking their time by using the above expression, among a host of others which indicate the same feeling.

senjitsu wa shitsurei shimashta
[*literally: I was rude the other day*]
This is used when meeting again after a fairly long interval. Westerners would thank their partner for

having had a marvellous time etc., but Japanese are likely to apologize.

However, when apologizing for having caused some real problem, Japanese rarely specify the reasons for this and just say 'I am sorry'. For example, when arriving late, they may say:

> **osoku natte, sumimasen**
> I am sorry that I'm late

while a Westerner often feels that a detailed explanation must be given as well.

It is good form to bow when apologizing, even to friends. This bow need not be deep, but it should be noticeable.

sort (*type*) shurui
a different sort of . . . chigau shurui no . . .

soup sūpu

south minami
in the south minami no

souvenir o-miyage
as a souvenir o-miyage toshte

speak hanasu /hanashimas/
do you speak English? Eigo o hanashimas ka?
may I speak English? Eigo o hanashte mo ī des ka?
I don't speak . . . . . . o hanashimasen
can I speak to . . .? (*on telephone*) . . . -san to hanashte mo ī des ka?
I wish I could speak Japanese Nihongo o hanasetara ī des

special tokubetsu (no)

speed (*noun*) spīdo
we'll try to speed things up spīdo o agete mimas

spoon spūn

spring (*season*) haru
in the spring haru ni

stairs kaidan

stamp (*postage*) kitte
two stamps for Great Britain, please Igirisu ate kitte ni-mai o-negai shimas

stand (*noun: at trade fair etc.*) uriba
at our stand watakshi-tachi no uriba de
at your stand anata no uriba de

start (*transitive*) hajimeru /hajimemas/
(*intransitive*) hajimaru /hajimarimas/
starting from next month raigetsu kara

station eki 駅

STATUS

Japanese are extremely status-conscious. Indeed, status is considerably more important than job content, qualifications etc. If you are in business your status in your organization should be clearly stated on your business card.

stay: I'm staying at . . . . . . ni tomatte imas

steal nusumu /nusumimas/
my suitcase has been stolen ryokō-kaban ga nusumare-mashta

sterling (*currency*) Igirisu pondo

sticking plaster bansōkō

still mada
it's still not right mada dame des
is it still open? mada aite imas ka?

stomach onaka

stomach-ache onaka no itami

stop (*road sign*) tomare 止まれ
(*intransitive*) tomaru /tomarimas/
(*transitive*) tomeru /tomemas/
could you stop here, please? (*to taxi driver etc.*) koko de tomatte kudasaimas ka?
does this train stop at . . .? kono densha wa . . . de tomarimas ka?

straight massugu
straight on massugu

strange hen (na)

stranger: I'm a stranger here watashi wa, kono hen wa wakarimasen

straw mat tatami

STRAW MATS

The **tatami** is a rectangular straw mat which is covered with a thin layer of woven rush. It is roughly the size of a bed: six feet long, three feet wide and up to three inches thick. In a Japanese-style room the floor is completely covered with such mats.

street michi
   the next street on the left hidari-te no tsugi no michi
   what street is it on? sore wa, dono michi des ka?

STREETS

Since streets in Japan, except some of the biggest ones, generally don't have names, it is more relevant to ask:

   which block is it in?
   sore wa, nan chōme des ka?
   could you write the street name down? michi no nam-e o kaite kudasaimas ka?
   could you write the number of the block down? nan-chōme ka kaite kudasaimas ka?

strike (*noun*) sto

string himo

strong (*material, drink*) tsuyoi
   (*taste*) koi

student gaksei

stupid baka (na)

successful seikō shta
   here's to a successful relationship! ots-ki-ai no sēkō o inotte!

suddenly totsuzen ni

sugar satō

suit (*noun: clothing*) sūtsu

suitcase ryokōkaban

summer natsu
   in the summer natsu ni

sun tai-yō

sun glasses san gurasu

sunburnt hi-yake shta

Sunday nichi-yō-bi

suntan lotion hi-yake rōshon

supper yūshoku

SUPPER *see* DINNER

supplier kyōkyū-sha

supply (*verb*) kyōkyū suru /kyōkyū shimas/

sure: I'm sure tashka des
  I'm not sure taska dewa arismasen
  are you sure? tashka des ka?

surname myōji

SURNAMES

Until about 1870, only those Japanese of noble birth had surnames. However, during the following Meiji Restoration commoners were allowed to adopt surnames as well.

A modern dictionary of Japanese names lists 13,000 surnames – in stark contrast to neighbouring China or Korea, where surnames re are far fewer in number. Most of them reflect the place where the family originally resided. For example:

Ta-naka	among the rice field(s)
Yama-naka	among the mountain(s)
Yama-moto	foot of the mountain
Ishi-moto	foot of the stone(s)
Ishi-da	stony rice field
Ta-mura	rice field village
Mura-matsu	village pine tree(s)
Matsu-sh'ta	under the pine tree(s)
Hon-da	main rice field
Kawa-bata	riverside
Hayashi	wood
Ko-bayashi	little wood
Kure-bayashi	crimson wood
Mori	forest
Ōmori	big forest
Ko-mori	little forest

For the correct use of surnames *see* ADDRESSING PEOPLE.

swearword warui kotoba

SWEARWORDS

With their great emphasis on politeness, especially towards Westerners, Japanese rarely admit to the existence of swearwords in their language, apart from the rather tame (to us, not to them!)

  baka!
  you fool!

and
>**chiku-shō**
>beast

Japanese insist that these and other **warui kotoba** (bad words) should not be divulged to outsiders. Language schools certainly don't teach them. Moving in middle-class society, one will rarely hear them, anyway. However, if you come in contact with workers during a bar-room brawl, you will hear far stronger words, though there is an absence of swearwords related to sex or excretory functions of the Anglo-American type.

Of course Japanese can be insulting in quite another way: with their many honorifics and elaborate verb endings (*see* POLITENESS LEVELS) all it needs for someone to be insulting is NOT to use the proper form required on a specific occasion. Conversely, one can also insult someone else by using a language which is consciously too polite!

swim oyogu /oyogimas/

swimming pool sui-ē pūru

switch (*noun: light switch, on machine etc.*) suittchi

SYLLABARIES

A syllabary is a system of writing Japanese without using Chinese ideograms. Japanese has two syllabaries: **Hiragana** and **Katakana** (*see* WRITING SYSTEM).

T

table tēburu
  See FURNITURE

take toru /torimas/
  I'll take it (*buy*) sore ni shimas
  how long does it take? (*journey, job*) dore kurai kakarimas ka?

talk hanasu /hanashimas/
  can I talk to . . . ? . . . -san to hanashte mo ī des ka?

tall (*person*) se ga takai
  (*building*) takai

tap ja-guchi

tape (*for tape-recorder*) tēpu

tape-recorder tēpu rekōdā

taxi takshī   タクシー

TAXIS

These days taxis are expensive, like almost everything else in Japan. However, the nickname **kamikaze driver** is no longer warranted, since drivers are now paid by the hour and not by the number of fares.

While there is no tipping of taxi drivers, late at night one may have to pay two to three times the fare indicated on the meter. Since subways and buses stop running rather early at night, except in Tokyo, this can cause problems, and taxi drivers can get choosy. Apparently the trick is to hold up two or three fingers on flagging down a a taxi to indicate a proposed doubling or tripling of the fare.

Since few taxi drivers know any English, and because the Japanese system of house addresses is complicated anyway, it is best to enter the taxi with your destination address clearly written or drawn on a piece of paper. If you stay at a hotel, somebody at the front desk (called **furonto**) will usually oblige.

Don't despair if the driver has to ask for directions at one or more police boxes on the way – this is quite normal!

The opening and closing of the passenger side of the rear door is operated by the driver – there is no need to do it yourself. Stand clear of this door before entering or after leaving the taxi!

Some words and phrases:

please call a taxi
takshī o yonde kudasai

please go to this address
kono jūsho ni itte kudasai

please go to X-hotel
X-hoteru ni itte kudasai

how much does it cost?
ikura des ka?

please go right
migi ni itte kudasai

please go left
hidari ni itte kudasai

please go straight on
massugu ni itte kudasai

please stop
tomatte kudasai

tea (*green*) o-cha　お茶
(*Indian*) kō'cha　　紅茶
a cup of tea ippai no o-cha

TEA

Japanese make a strict distinction between Indian tea (**kō-cha**) and Japanese or green tea (**o-cha**).

While the former is offered with the usual Western additions of milk, sugar, clatter of spoons and saucers etc., **o-cha** is drunk from cups without handles, and without any additives.

Like tea for the British, **o-cha** keeps Japanese cool in summer and hot in winter, peps them up and relaxes them – it is, in short, a drink for all occasions. Before your talk with the bank manager or equivalent, a charming girl will come and serve **o-cha** to all persons present in his office, often with a tiny piece of beautifully sculpted confectionery (**o-kashi**), which can be sweetness incarnate.

These days, large vacuum flasks unfortunately tend to replace the charming servers of **o-cha** in more mundane establishments. The tea ceremony has made a very strict ritual of the serving of Japanese tea, emphasizing the inherent simplicity of the act and the equality of all those who take part. Be warned, though, that you will be thinking much

more about your aching legs than about the beauty
of tea during such a ceremony.

teacher sensei

Although this term most often refers to educators, it
is a respectful form of address for professionals in
other fields too: doctors, dentists, lawyers and writers
may all be referred to or directly addressed as **sensei**.
Since it is a term of respect, it is not usually used to
refer to oneself, the more neutral **kyōshi** being used
instead:

> **I'm a teacher**
> kyōshi des

teahouse cha-mise

telegram dempō

telephone (*noun*) denwa
(*verb*) denwa suru /denwa shimas/
> **can I use your telephone?** denwa o tskatte mo ī des
> ka?

telephone directory denwa-chō

TELEPHONES

Japanese public phones are ubiquitous, come in
many shapes and colours – and, above all, actually
work! Furthermore, for the price of 10 Yen (a little
over 4p) you can phone the length and breadth of
Tokyo or Osaka. However, long-distance calls are
more expensive than in Europe. No wonder, then,
that Japanese spend long periods talking to each
other over the phone, often bowing to their invisible
partner. One of the first words you are likely to hear
in Japan is **moshi-moshi!** (our 'hello!') as someone is
phoning.

Here are some useful phrases:

> **is Mr/Mrs . . . available, please?**
> . . . -san ga irrasshaimas ka?

> **this is Smith**
> Sumisu des

> **Is that Mr Tanaka?**
> Tanaka-san des ka?

> **yes, it's me speaking**
> hai, watakshi des

> **I'll call back later**
> ato de denwa shimas

when will he be back?
itsu kare wa modorimas ka?

please say Mr . . . called
. . . kara denwa datta to shirasete kudasai

Typical responses you may hear are:

moshi-moshi
hello

donata deshō ka?
who's calling please?

o-machi kudasai
hold on please

kare wa rusu des
he's not here

dengon ga arimas ka?
can I take a message?

During the conversation Japanese require far more interjections, such as **hai-hai, sō deska** etc., to make sure that their partner is still following the conversation. You might, therefore, also sometimes get an anxious **moshi-moshi** if you have been quiet for too long.

television terebi

telex terekksu

temperature (*fever*) netsu
(*of body*) taion

temple tera

terms (*of contract*) jōken

terrible hidoi

than . . . . . . yori

To say '**A is . . . than B**' use the pattern:
A wa B yori . . . des

While English uses 'more' or '-er', Japanese uses the simple adjective:

big ōkī

A is bigger than B
A wa B yori ōkī des

good ī

this one's better than that
kore wa sore yori ī des

thank you arigatō
thank you very much dōmo arigatō gozaimashta
no thank you kekkō des

See also PLEASE, SORRY

that sono/ano; sore/are

The first pair are adjectives and come directly before the noun. **Sono** refers to something close, **ano** refers to something far away. For example:

>**that man** (*just behind you*) sono hito
>(*over there*) ano hito

The same distinction holds for the second pair, which are pronouns:

>**what is that?** (*near you*) sore wa nan des ka?
>(*over there*) are wa nan des ka?

that's for you sore wa anata ni des

can I have that one? sore o totte mo ī des ka?

Note that Japanese can use these same words to mean 'those' as well as 'that'.

the

There is no word in Japanese corresponding to 'the' (*see* A, AN).

theatre gekijō

their karera no; *see* PERSONAL PRONOUNS

theirs karera no; *see* PERSONAL PRONOUNS

them karera o; *see* PERSONAL PRONOUNS

then (*after that*) sore-kara
(*at that time*) sono toki

there (*if nearby*) soko
(*over there*) asoko

I want that one there (*near you*) soko no ga hoshī des
(*over there*) asoko no ga hoshī des

For 'there is' and 'there are' Japanese has two expressions depending on whether you are talking about people or things:

>**there is/are ...** (*referring to people*) ... imas
>(*referring to things*) ... arimas
>**is/are there ... ?** (*referring to people*) ... imas ka?
>(*referring to things*) ... arimas ka?

these (*adjective*) korera no
(*pronoun*) korera

As plurals do not figure much in Japanese grammar, the use of these two translations is not that common. **Kono** or **kore** can be used instead (*see* **this**) and the idea of plurality is inferred from context.

they karera wa/ga; *see* PERSONAL PRONOUNS

thick (*plank*) atsui
  (*soup*) koi

thin (*person*) yaseta
  (*thing*) usui

thing mono
  (*abstract*) koto

think kangaeru /kangaemas/
  what do you think? dō omoimas ka?
  I think so sō omoimas
  I don't think so sō omoimasen
  we'll have to think about it sore ni tsuite kangae-nakute wa narimasen

thirsty nodo ga kawaita
  I'm very thirsty totemo nodo ga kawaite imas

this (*adjective*) kono
  (*pronoun*) kore
  this visit kono hōmon
  this photograph kono shashin
  can I have this one? kore o totte mo ī des ka?
  is this yours? kore wa anata no des ka?
  this is Mr O'Hara (*introducing him*) kochira wa O'Hara-san des

those (*adjective*) sorera no/arera no/
  (*pronoun*) sorera/arera/
  It is more common in Japanese to use the singular form rather than these words. For more on this, and for the difference between these words, *see* **that**.

throat nodo

through . . . . . . o tōtte
  through Tokyo Tōkyō o tōtte

Thursday moku-yō-bi

ticket (*for cinema, train*) kippu

tie (*clothing*) nektai

TIES
Japanese businessmen tend to be more formal than their Western counterparts, in their dress as in other ways. Even in the atrociously muggy summer weather, ties and jackets are not discarded when other cultures (such as Singapore or Hong Kong Chinese) who suffer from a similar climate will have introduced open-neck shirts or safari suits.

In keeping with this, it hardly needs special mention that ties should not be too loud and flashy.

tight (*schedule*) konde iru
(*fit, clothes*) kitsui

tights taitsu

time jikan
there's not much time amari jikan ga arimasen
we've plenty of time jikan wa jūbun arimas
last time zenkai ni
next time jikai ni
what's the time? nanji des ka?

TIME

To tell the time, Japanese use the Chinese-derived numbers (*see* COUNTING OBJECTS), adding **-ji** for 'o'clock' and **-fun** or **-pun** for 'minute':

one o'clock	ichi-ji
five o'clock	go-ji

Officially, the 24-hour system is in use, where 10 p.m. is 22 hours, etc. However, informally the system is similar to the British one:

10 a.m.	asa jū-ji (asa = morning)
	gozen jū-ji (gozen = before noon)
8.15 p.m.	gogo hachi-ji jūgo-fun (gogo = afternoon)

Half past is **-han**:

7.30 p.m.	gogo shichi-ji-han [*literally: p.m. seven hour half*]

or (officially):

jū-ku-ji-han [*literally: ten nine nine hour half*]

Here are examples of time expressions:

3.00 p.m.	gogo san-ji
3.10 p.m.	gogo san-ji-juppun
3.15 p.m.	gogo san-ji-jūgo-fun
3.20 p.m.	gogo san-ji-ni-juppun
3.25 p.m.	gogo san-ji-ni-jū-go-fun
3.30 p.m.	gogo san-ji-han
3.35 p.m.	gogo san-ji-san-jūgo-fun
3.50 p.m.	gogo san-ji-go-juppun

As can be seen from the above, you can tell the time in Japanese without using equivalents for the English 'past' and 'to'. Such words do exist though:

| **sugi** | past |
| **mae** | to |

Both are used after the expression giving the minutes:

| **10.20** | jū-ji nijuppun sugi |
| **7.50** | hachi-ji juppun mae |

timetable (*for travel*) jikoku-hyō

tip (*to waiter etc.*) chippu

TIPPING
There is no tipping in Japan, except perhaps in clip joints for Western tourists who feel uncomfortable if they haven't tipped the waiters. Don't let this bad habit spread!

tired tsukarete
   I'm tired tsukarete imas

tissues tisshū pēpā

TISSUES
Tissues are widely used in Japan, especially for wiping one's hands in public conveniences, which generally do not provide any cloth or paper towels. However, there are sometimes vending machines for tissues inside such places. Luxury hotels should provide towels, but it is best not to bank on it, and to carry tissues or a handkerchief.

Loud blowing of one's nose into tissues is not considered polite, while sniffling is tolerated to an amazing degree. If you absolutely must use tissues for blowing your nose (far better than using a handkerchief), try to do it out of earshot (admittedly difficult!) or, at least, turn your back on the assembled company. *See also* HANDKERCHIEFS.

to . . . . . . ni
   to London Rondon ni
   to . . . Hotel, please . . . hoteru ni, o-negai shimas

toast (*drinking*) kampai

TOASTS
With much clinking of glasses, Japanese toasts are similar to Western ones. **Kampai** means 'dry (i.e. empty) the cup'. Japanese will often want to know the equivalent expression from other countries from you – an auspicious start for repeated (reciprocal)

pourings of **sake**, beer, whisky or whatever. Don't pour your own drink, and raise your glass if somebody pours for you.

tobacco tabako

today kyō

toe ashi no yubi

together issho ni
    can we pay together? issho ni haratte mo ī des ka?

toilet toire トイレ
    can I use your toilet? toire o tskatte mo ī des ka?
    where is the toilet? toire wa doko des ka?

toilet paper toiretto pēpā

TOILETS

These days you will mostly come across Western-style toilets, which should not present any problems. Just watch out if there are special toilet slippers (usually marked **WC**) outside or just inside the toilet door and put them on, leaving your regular slippers outside.

In case of a Japanese-style toilet, squat over it, facing the water container. This does not encourage the reading of novels, but is more hygienic, in case you are worried about unclean toilet seats. In most houses you will find a little towel for drying your hands after washing them in the hollow at the top of the water container, where the supply pipe curves down. In many other places there is no provision for drying your hands (except in luxury hotels), so always carry some tissues or a handkerchief with you for this purpose (*see also* TISSUES, HANDKERCHIEFS).

tomorrow ashta
    tomorrow morning ashta no asa
    tomorrow evening ashta no ban
    the day after tomorrow asatte

ton ton

tongue shta

tonight kon-ya

too (*excessively*) . . . -sugiru
    (*also*) mo
    it's too expensive sore wa taka-sugimas
    me too watakshi mo sō des

The suffix **-sugiru** can be added to adjectives or verbs. In the case of adjectives, remove the final **-i** or **na** and add **-sugiru** (or more politely **-sugimas**):

> **it's too hot**
> atsu-sugimas

In the case of verbs, add the suffix to the basic stem (*see* VERBS):

> **I drank too much**
> nomi-sugimashta
> **I ate too much**
> tabe-sugimashta

tooth ha

toothache ha-ita

toothbrush ha-burashi

toothpaste neri-hamigaki

top (*of box etc.*) u-e

total (*noun*) gōkei

tour (*noun*) ryokō

tourist ryokō-sha

towel ta-oru

town machi
 in town machi ni

trade fair bus-san-ten

tradition dentō

TRADITION

Although Japan may look thoroughly westernized on the surface, this should not lead to the conclusion that the way of thinking is also like ours. One fundamental difference is that Westerners are imbued with two thousand years of Christianity, which basically stresses individualism, while the Japanese have been very little influenced by it. Instead, for thousands of years they have been shaped by the interaction of Shintō native religion and Confucian ethics. In Japan the smallest unit has therefore traditionally not been the individual, but the family group, and every person saw him- or herself first and foremost as a member of such a group.

In Japan (unlike traditional China) it has been possible to invoke this feeling of family unity with unrelated persons as well, so that other groupings, such as business concerns, make strong use of this concept. Very often, of course, all this 'togetherness' may be a sham, but on the surface it is important to pretend that it exists. Preservation of harmony (**wa**) is invoked time and again, together with other traditional virtues, to strengthen group solidarity and to guard against the deviations of individuals.

While some present-day Japanese, especially those who have lived in the West, may rail against this tradition, most others feel secure in it. Being Japanese, traditions provide them with integrated patterns of thinking and behaviour which are successful in a fast-changing world. Unlike, say, African tribal society, Japanese tradition has paradoxically proved to be a mainstay in the rapid industrialization and modernization of the country.

While Westerners may love or hate Japanese traditions, they cannot themselves become true Japanese, owing to their far greater insistence on individualism. However, there is a great potential for trying to understand Japanese traditions by living in Japan with an open mind and by trying to see a little of it through Japanese eyes.

traditional dentō-teki (na)

train densha

translate hon-yaku suru /hon-yaku shimas/
  could you translate? hon-yaku shte kudasaimas ka?

translation hon-yaku

translator hon-yaku-sha

travel ryokō suru /shimas/

travel agency ryokō dairiten　旅行代理店

traveller's cheque ryokō-gitte

tree ki

tremendous mono-sugoi

trial period kokoromi no jiki

trousers zubon

true hontō no
  that's true sore wa hontō des
  that's not true sore wa hontō dewa arimasen

trust shin-yō suru /shimas/
  we must trust each other otagai ni shin-yō shinakereba narimasen

try yatte miru /yatte mimas/
   we'll try yatte mimas

Tuesday ka-yō-bi

turnover (*of business*) uri-age-daka

twice nibai

typewriter taipuraitā

typhoon taifū

tyre taiya

U

ugly mi-nikui

umbrella kasa

uncle (*own uncle*) oji
  (*someone else's*) oji-san

under (*spatially*) . . . no shta ni
  (*less than*) . . . miman

understand wakaru /wakarimas/
  I don't understand wakarimasen
  I understand wakarimas

United States Beikoku   米国

unusual mezurashī

up ue ni [oo-eh]
  this way up (*package*) kochira o ue ni
  sales are up uri-age ga agarimas

upstairs ue [oo-eh]

urgent kink'yū (no)

us watakshi-tachi no; *see* PERSONAL PRONOUNS

use tsukau /tsukaimas/
  can I use . . . ? . . . o tsukatte mo ī des ka?

useful yaku ni tatsu

usually futsū

V

valid (*passport, contract*) yūkō (na)

valuable kichō (na)

vegetarian (*person*) saishoku shugisha

VERBS

All main verbs in Japanese come at the end of the
sentence, and remain the same regardless of number
or person. Thus, in:

    Igirisu-jin des
    I am English/he is English etc.

the verb **des** could mean 'I am', 'you are', 'he is', 'we
are', etc. The correct meaning in each case will
usually be clear from context.

Every verb in Japanese has both polite forms and
plain forms, the former being used in ordinary polite
conversation, the latter being reserved for casual
speech with family, close friends, small children etc.
In this book, both forms are given, the plain (or
'dictionary') form first, followed by the polite form
(e.g. go **iku** /**ikimas**/).

The various polite endings are:

-mas	*present positive*
-masen	*present negative*
-mashta	*past positive*
-masen deshta	*past negative*

For example:

ikimas	I go
ikimasen	I don't go
ikimashta	I went
ikimasen deshta	I didn't go

Only one verb, **des**, cannot take these endings – see
below, under EXCEPTIONS TO PATTERNS A, B, C.

The plain (present positive) form, on the other
hand, always ends in **-u**:

taberu	I eat
nomu	I drink

Although they have the same ending, these two
verbs do in fact belong to two different categories, or
types. Indeed, 'all' verbs belong to one of two types:
those whose plain form ends in **-eru** or **-iru** (e.g.

taberu, a Type 1 verb) and those whose plain form doesn't (e.g. **nomu,** a Type 2 verb).

In fact, six verbs ending in **-iru** and one verb ending in **-eru** are exceptions and follow the Type 2 pattern instead. These are **hairu** (enter), **hashiru** (run), **kiru** (cut), **shiru** (know), **kagiru** (limit), **iru** (need) and **kaeru** (return). There are also three verbs which belong to neither type: *see* EXCEPTIONS below.

We have seen that all Type 1 verbs end in either **-iru** or **-eru.** Type 2 verbs, on the other hand, have eight possible endings besides the **-mu** of **nomu** (drink). Examples of these eight are **yobu** (call), **shinu** (die), **nugu** (take off), **uru** (sell), **arau** (wash), **kaku** (write), **hanasu** (speak) and **matsu** (wait).

The reason for dividing all Japanese verbs into two great classes is that all the verb patterns you will need can be generated once it is known to which of the two types a verb belongs. We shall concentrate on three main patterns: A, B, and C.

PATTERN A

This, the most important pattern, gives us the *basic stem,* from which we make simple polite verbs and verbs of wanting and suggesting.

Type 1: remove **-ru** (e.g. **mi-, tabe-**)

Type 2: change **-su** to **-shi** (e.g. **hanashi-**)*
change **tsu** to **-chi** (e.g. **machi-**)

and for all others

change **-u** to **-i** (e.g. **nomi-, yobi-** etc.)

*This final **-i-** of the stem disappears before a **-t.**

To this basic stem, you add the following suffixes:

	positive	negative
simple present	-mas	-masen
simple past	-mashta	-masen deshta
want present	-tai des	-taku nai des or -taku arimasen
want past	-takatta des	-taku nakatta des or -taku arimasen deshta
suggestion ('let's . . .')	-mashō	---

For example:

sushi o tabemas
I eat sushi

nani mo mimasen deshta
I saw nothing

bīru ga nomitai des
I want to drink some beer

machitaku nakatta des
I didn't want to wait

urimashō
let's sell it

PATTERN B

This pattern gives us the *participle form*, necessary in generating progressive tenses ('is doing' etc.), polite commands ('do it, please' etc.) and requests of various kinds ('could you do it, please?', 'may I . . .' etc.):

Type 1: add **-te** to the basic stem (e.g. **mite, tabete**)

Type 2: make the following changes from the plain form:

-mu, -bu, -nu to **-nde**
(e.g. **nonde, yonde, shinde**)

-ru, -tsu, (vowel **u**) **u** to **-tte**
(e.g. **utte, matte, aratte**)

-gu to **-ide** (e.g. **nuide**)
-ku to **-ite*** (e.g. **kaite**)
-su to **-shte** (e.g. **hanashte**)

*One exception: **iku** becomes **itte**.

The participle can be used in combination with the following:

	positive	negative
progressive present	u imas	u imasen
progressive past	u imashta	u imasen deshta
polite commands	u kudasai	---
requests (of others)	u kuremasen ka?	---
requests (for self)	u mo ī des ka?	---
must not	u wa ikemasen	---

For example:

nani o tabete imas ka?
what are you eating?

asoko de matte imashta
I was waiting over there

eigo de hanashte kudasai
please speak English

eigo de hanashte kuremasen ka?
could you speak in English please?

mado o akete mo ī des ka?
may I open the window?

aratte wa ikemasen
you mustn't wash it

PATTERN C

Based as it is on Pattern B, this pattern is very easily formed: just change the final **-e** of the participle to **-a**: **mita, tabeta, nonda, hanashta**, etc.

In fact, these are plain past forms, so they should not be used as main verbs except in very informal speech. However, combined with other phrases, they are very useful (for an explanation of their formation *see* PLAIN FORMS).

	positive	*negative*
'have (ever) done'	**u koto ga arimas**	**u koto ga arimasen**
'had done'	**u koto ga arimashta**	**u koto ga arimasen deshta**
'after . . . ing'	**u ato de**	---
'should'	**u hō ga ī des**	---
'should have'	**u hō ga yokatta des**	---

For example:

sashimi o tabeta koto ga arimas ka?
have you (ever) eaten sashimi?

Fuji-san ni nobotta koto ga arimasen
I haven't (ever) climbed Mt Fuji

tabeta ato de
after eating

sugu uchi ni kaetta hō ga ī des
you should go home straight away

tegami o kaita hō ga yokatta des ne
I should have written the letter, shouldn't I?

EXCEPTIONS TO PATTERNS A, B, C:

Two very common verbs, **suru** (do) and **kuru** (come), are irregular in some of their forms:

	SURU	KURU
PATTERN A	shi-*	ki-
PATTERN B	shte	kite
PATTERN C	shta	kita

For example:

shimasen deshta
I didn't do it

kite kudasai
please come

*This -i- disappears before a -t:

shtai des
I want to do it

Note also that **des** (be, plain form **da**) has the following forms:

	positive	negative
present (polite)	**des**	**de wa arimasen**
(plain)	**da**	**de wa nai**
past (polite)	**deshta**	**de wa arimasen deshta**
(plain)	**datta**	**de wa nakatta**

and **de wa** often becomes **ja** (i.e. **ja arimasen** etc.).

very totemo, taihen
  very good totemo yoi
  I like it very much sore ga totemo ski des
  very tired taihen tsukareta

village mura

visa biza

visit (*noun*) hōmon
  we enjoyed our visit tanoshku sugoshimashta

VISITS

While Japanese tend to apologize at the end of a visit for having caused trouble (*see* SORRY), it is quite all right for Westerners to thank Japanese hosts in the way given above. *See also* HOSPITALITY.

voice ko-e

VOICE

Because of the various politeness levels, Japanese voices can change dramatically, depending on whether they are used for talking to a superior, a friend, or an inferior.

A hesitant tone to express one's reserve is important when one wants to be polite.

Tone of voice is trained when newcomers join a large firm every spring. Special classes are held, especially in the 'correct' way to answer the telephone or to greet customers. A good place to listen to a very polite tone of voice (which might sound rather artificial to Westerners) is to ride the lifts (**erebētā**) of prestigious department stores (**depāto**) with the 'elevator girl' (**erebētā gāru**), who calls out the floors' merchandise with unfailing sweetness of voice.

Sudden change in tone can be witnessed when in a room with a Japanese who is phoning, in quick succession, persons with high and low status.

By comparison, no matter how hard they may try, most Westerners speaking Japanese tend to sound too forthright and therefore rather rude. However, allowances are made (mostly unconsciously), for if a Westerner were to talk Japanese with a perfectly modulated tone of voice, this would sound rather affected.

Needless to say, a sweet tone of voice is much more important in the case of females. Males, on the other hand, especially with their inferiors or their wives, are expected to sound somewhat abrupt and a little rough – this reinforces their manly image (**otoko-rashī imēji**).

volcano kazan

W

wait (*verb*) matsu /machimas/
    don't wait for me matanaide kudasai
    wait for me matte kudasai
    I'll wait for you anata o machimas
    I'm waiting for someone (*e.g. said to waiter*) dar-ka o matte imas

waiter uētā
    waiter! chotto! (This is not the translation of 'waiter', but is a very useful word meaning 'a little', which can be used to attract attention in many situations.)

waitress uētores

Wales U-ēruzu

walk (*verb*) aruku /arukimas/
    let's walk there soko made arukimashō

wall kabe

wallet saifu

want hoshī
    This word is an adjective:

        I want X
        X ga hoshī des
        [*literally: X (object particle) is desired*]

        that's not what I want
        sore wa hoshī mono ja arimasen

        what do you want?
        nani ga hoshī des ka?

    'Want to' with a verb is something quite different. Add **-tai** to the verb stem (*see* VERBS):

        I want to go
        ikitai

        I want to buy it
        kaitai

    To make these sentences negative change **-i** to **-ku nai**:

        I don't want to go
        ikitaku nai

        I don't want to buy it
        kaitaku nai

All these forms can be made more polite by adding
des (ikitai des etc.).

warm (*climate, day, person*) atatakai

was *see* BE

wash (*verb*) arau /araimas/

watch (*wristwatch*) ude-dokei

water mizu　水
　cold water o-hiya
　hot water o-yu
　a glass of water, please mizu o ippai o-negai shimas

way (*direction*): which is the way to . . . ? . . . yuki no
michi wa dore des ka?

we watakshi-tachi
　See PERSONAL PRONOUNS

weak (*material*) yowai

weather tenki
　what weather! (*very good*) nante subarashī tenki nan
　deshō!
　(*very bad*) nante hidoi tenki nan deshō!

WEATHER

The greatest single influence on the Japanese
weather is the prevailing wind direction. During
summer, south-easterly winds blow from the Pacific,
causing it to be hot and very humid, while in winter
the north-westerly winds from Siberia are very cold
and relatively dry. The latter unload most of their
moisture in the form of heavy snowfalls on the
mountains of the Japan Sea coast (north-west), while
south-eastern parts (which include the major cities)
then receive dry, cold air.

Japanese often show pride in the fact that the
country has four quite distinct seasons – as opposed
to the British climatic vagaries. A case can be made
that there are really five seasons:

Spring, between March and May, is much like
European spring, although with less extreme recur-
rences of winter cold. This is the time for viewing
cherry and plum blossoms.

It is followed by a hot and extremely rainy period
(called the **tsu yu** – literally: plum rains) between
early June and the middle of July. It is during this
time that the rice fields need to get their vital water
for adequate irrigation.

Between the middle of July and the end of September the weather, though still very muggy, becomes less rainy. Towards September typhoons are likely to strike the country, especially its southern provinces.

Autumn follows, with cooler, dry weather, which can be most pleasant and which lasts right into December. This is the time for outings to observe the leaves changing colour.

Winter arrives with heavy snowfalls in some parts of the country, though the major cities experience this only rarely. While winter is mostly crisp and sunny, cloudy skies can make things unpleasant if you live in a draughty, unheated Japanese house.

wedding kekkon
wedding ceremony kekkon-shki

WEDDINGS

A Japanese wedding tends to be a grandiose affair, since it represents the linking of two families in perpetuity. No expense is to be spared, and owners of 'marriage palaces' grow rich on the inability of the couple and their parents to decline extra frills during the great day – the face of the family is at stake.

Something similar occurs during Western funerals – who is going to skimp on the de-luxe casket for the Dearly Beloved, although everyone knows how little use is made of it?

Since marriage is still primarily a vehicle for the continuation of the family, it is natural that it should be such a grand day, with bride and groom often seeming no more than passive puppets.

The guest list commonly includes a large number of business associates of the groom, rather than personal friends of the couple.

Wednesday sui-yō-bi

week: one week isshūkan
  two weeks nishūkan
  this week konshū
  next week raishū
  last week senshū
  every week maishū

weekend shūmatsu
  at the weekend shūmatsu ni

WEEKENDS
Since Japan is a non-Christian country, Sundays were traditionally not a day of rest. However, schools and large firms do close on Sundays, many also on Saturday afternoons, though the long weekend is not yet generally established. On the other hand, shops do a lot of their business on Sundays and tend to be closed on one other day of the week (often Mondays). To present a slightly less intense 'workaholic' image to the world, large companies (e.g. banks) are currently being urged to introduce Saturdays as days of rest as well.

weight omosa

welcome: you're welcome dō itashimashte
    thank you for your very warm welcome kangei shte kudasai-mashte makoto ni

well (*in health*) yoi
    not well (*in health*) yoku nai
    are you well? o-genki des ka?
    I'm very well, thank you (*as response*) genki des, dōmo
    things are going well umaku itte imas
    you speak English extremely well Eigo ga o-jōzu des, nē

were *see* BE

west nishi
    in the west (*direction*) nishi ni
    in the West (*Europe and America*) Ōbei ni

Western-style yōshiki

wet: it's wet nurete imas

whale kujira

what? nan des ka?
    what is that? are wa nan des ka?

wheel sha-rin

when? itsu des ka?
    when does it start? itsu hajimarimas ka?
    (*at the time when*) . . . toki
    when I bought it katta toki

where? doko des ka?
    where is it? sore wa doko des ka?

which
This can be either an adjective or a pronoun.

adjective
    (*which of two*) **dochira no**
    (*which of several*) **dono**

> **dochira no kokeshi ga hoshī des ka?**
> which (of the two) doll(s) do you want?

> **dono kokeshi ga hoshī des ka?**
> which (of the several) doll(s) do you want?

pronoun
    (*which one of two*) **dochira**
    (*which one of several*) **dore**

> **dochira ga hayai des ka?**
> which is the faster?

> **dore ga ichiban hayai des ka?**
> which is the fastest?

> **dore des ka?**
> which (one)?

whisky uiskī

white shiroi

white-collar worker sararī-man

who? (*plain form*) dare des ka?
    (*polite form*) donata des ka?
    (*very polite*) donata-sama des ka?

why? naze des ka?
    why not? (*of course*) mochiron des
    (*in response to suggestion*) **yes, why not?** ī ja nai ka?

wide hiroi

wife (*own: plain form*) kanai
    (*someone else's: polite form*) ok-san
    (*someone else's: very polite*) uku-sama

WIFE

If, as in Japan, a marriage is primarily between two families (*see* WEDDINGS), a good wife's major function is to fulfil her duties adequately and to bear the children required for the continuation of the familiy line. Since the Second World War, new ideas, such as Western individualism, have naturally spread, but a lot of Japanese men still regard the function of a wife rather in the same way as a Western manager regards the function of an efficient secretary. Loving each other and happiness are not all-important:

laudable, if they develop after marriage, but not a precondition.

In traditional Japan most people were farmers. On a farm a wife has many important functions and usually contributes to the earning of money. However, samurai families often tended to treat their nubile daughters like pawns in a chess game, marrying them off to create favourable family alliances. The daughter's wishes were rarely taken into consideration. The modern Japan middle class has adopted many of the samurai ideals. An important one is the assumption that a woman should not work outside the home after marriage. Instead, she should devote herself full-time to the education of her children.

This has led to a very strong role differentiation in the family, with the man working outside it most of the time, thereby providing money and status, while the wife manages the money and is a powerful force inside the house. While Western observers may decry such a state, Japanese women often reply that being a wife is better than being a commuting 'salaryman'.

will *see* FUTURE TENSE

wind (*noun*) kaze

window mado
   a window seat, please mado-giwa no seki o o-negai shimas

wine budōshu

winter fuyu
   in the winter fuyu ni

with (*using*) . . . de
   with a knife naifu de
   (*accompanying*) . . . to issho ni
   can I go with you? anata to issho ni itte mo ī des ka?
   I went with Mr Tanaka Tanaka-san to issho ni ikimashta
   with milk miruku iri
   I don't have it with me motte imasen

without . . . nashi de
   without sugar satō nashi de

woman onna no hito

WOMEN

With different attitudes towards Western-inspired individualism (*see* TRADITION) and the role of a wife (*see* WEDDINGS, WIFE), it is not surprising that the status of women in Japanese society should be markedly different from that in the West.

While Western idealism makes couples believe that they are somehow unique, Japanese pragmatism looks for the absence of disabilities in both men and women who search for a partner. An analogy could be helpful: while, say, French gourmets might be very particular about the label and age of a wine they wish to drink with a certain meal, thus looking for uniqueness in the combination, Americans, on choosing a bottle of Coca-Cola, will not insist on a certain year of manufacture, or specific area where it was bottled. Instead, they will inspect the bottle and drink it if obvious faults are absent.

Japanese tend to place greater stress on the proper fulfilling of role expectations than Westerners. The role prescription for women (as well as for men) tends to be clear-cut in Japan, and it is difficult to break out unless they either have a very strong character or leave Japan for a Western environment.

Middle-class girls should therefore ideally graduate from a junior college. Some higher education is desired, so that one day they can be good teachers of their children, but they should not compete with their husbands, who tend to be university graduates.

During their work for a few years in some large company they start to prepare themselves for marriage by taking, for example, flower arrangement classes to attain the right composure. Overseas trips with the purpose of learning English are also a good preparation, as long as they don't have a love affair with a foreigner during that time.

Their marriage at the age of a maximum of twenty-five years will be followed by their first child, which is ideally born nine months later – a 'honeymoon baby'. One more child will follow after an interval of about two years, and then the new family is complete.

The wife's middle years will be spent educating the children, which is a full-time occupation in a country where academic achievement is is stressed so highly. Once her children have left the home, a great feeling of emptiness may be felt, which is often filled by attending further education classes. Since the husband is away so often, there is little chance for a strong couple relationship to develop.

Indeed, with longer life expectancy, Japanese women face a bleak future once they no longer have their children to care for. However, high land prices force children to build their house on the plot of the parents' house, so that older people live cheek-by-jowl with their offspring. Since babysitters are unknown in Japan, grandmothers have a continuing role to play in this respect, especially in the countryside and in small towns.

This description is naturally very general, but it tries to show the typical role of a modern Japanese woman.

Although legally equal, Japanese women's status is below that of males. However, psychologically, she can gain high status by making her husband and children dependent on her. In psychological parlance this is called 'vicarious living', i.e. the mother living her life through her children, especially her eldest son. Since being in the limelight is not a great craving of most Japanese, she can wield considerable power in the background, and those in the know will tacitly acknowledge her status.

wood (*material*) mokuzai

wool yōmō

word kotoba
 what is the word for . . . ? . . . wa dō īmas ka?

WORD ORDER
Although different from English, Japanese word order is relatively simple and constant. While English generally has:

 subject – verb – object

Japanese generally has:

 subject – object – verb

For example:

 kanai wa kimono o kau tsumori des
 my wife – kimono – intends to buy

This may be extended to:

 other material – subject – indirect object – direct object – verb

For example:

> **kesa shujin ga kanojo ni okane o agemashta**
> this morning – my husband – to her – money –
> gave

Forming questions does not affect the word order –
just add **ka**:

> **kesa shujin ga kanojo ni okane o agemashta ka?**
> did my husband give her the money this morn-
> ing?

It is a common rule that the general precedes the
particular; for example:

> **ashta no gogo san-ji ni**
> tomorrow – afternoon – three hours – at

work (*noun*) shigoto
  it's a lot of work taksan no shigoto des
  it's not working (*machine etc.*) kowarete imas

worry: don't worry shimpai shinaide kudasai

worse issō warui

wrestling puro-res
  (*Japanese-style*) sumō

write kaku /kakimas/
  could you write it down? sore o kaite kudasaimas ka?

writing: Japanese writing Nihon kakikata
  syllabic writing (*cursive*) hiragana
  syllabic writing (*square*) katakana
  ideographic writing kanji
  Western writing rāmaji

WRITING SYSTEM

Experts agree that the Japanese writing system is the
most difficult in the world. This is due to the fact
that over 1,200 years ago the Japanese, who had no
writing system of their own, came across the many
thousands of Chinese pictorial characters or ideographs (called **kanji** – literally: Chinese letters – in
Japanese) and adapted them to their own use. This is
rather like pushing a square peg into a round hole
for two major reasons:

  (a) Most Japanese **kanji** have more than one
pronunciation, usually two or three, with a maximum of about ten, depending on which word they
are used to represent. Chinese has only one pronunciation per ideograph. This means that rote memori-

あ *a*	か *ka*	さ *sa*	た *ta*	な *na*
い *i*	き *ki*	し *shi*	ち *chi*	に *ni*
う *u*	く *ku*	す *su*	つ *tsu*	ぬ *nu*
え *e*	け *ke*	せ *se*	て *te*	ね *ne*
お *o*	こ *ko*	そ *so*	と *to*	の *no*

は *ba*	ま *ma*	や *ya*	ら *ra*	わ *wa*	
ひ *bi*	み *mi*		り *ri*		
ふ *fu*	む *mu*	ゆ *yu*	る *ru*		
へ *be*	め *me*		れ *re*		
ほ *bo*	も *mo*	よ *yo*	ろ *ro*	を *(w)o*	ん *n*

The Hiragana alphabet

ア *a*	カ *ka*	サ *sa*	タ *ta*	ナ *na*
イ *i*	キ *ki*	シ *shi*	チ *chi*	ニ *ni*
ウ *u*	ク *ku*	ス *su*	ツ *tsu*	ヌ *nu*
エ *e*	ケ *ke*	セ *se*	テ *te*	ネ *ne*
オ *o*	コ *ko*	ソ *so*	ト *to*	ノ *no*

ハ *ha*	マ *ma*	ヤ *ya*	ラ *ra*	ワ *wa*	
ヒ *hi*	ミ *mi*		リ *ri*		
フ *fu*	ム *mu*	ユ *yu*	ル *ru*		
ヘ *he*	メ *me*		レ *re*		
ホ *ho*	モ *mo*	ヨ *yo*	ロ *ro*	ヲ *(w)o*	ン *n*

The Katakana alphabet

zation of **kanji** readings in their specific context is necessary.

(b) Unlike Chinese (but like English), many Japanese words change their shape, especially their endings, depending on tense etc. For example:

English	I arrive	I am arriving	I arrived
Japanese	**tsu-ki-mas**	**tsu-ite-imas**	**tsu-ki-mashta**
Chinese	**dao**	**dao**	**dao**

The ideograph for 'arriving' is 着く. This is all that Chinese needs, since tense is inferred from context only, and only one way of pronouncing this will be necessary. If we tried to write English with Chinese characters, we would also have to write 着く with something following it, for example 着く ing, 着く ed etc.

This is the reason why the **kana** syllabaries developed in the following centuries. They are separate phonetic scripts and both of them can produce all the sounds of the Japanese language. **Hiragana** (the more rounded one) is normally used in conjunction with **kanji**, as in the case of 'arriving' shown above. The square **katakana** is used for writing the many loan words from Western languages (especially English), for emphasis, or for other technical reasons.

Currently, Japanese is thus written with a combination of four different systems: an official list for general use of about 2,000 **kanji** (going up to about 4,000 in specialist academic writings), the two phonetic systems **hiragana** and **katakana**, each containing forty-eight symbols, as well as the Western alphabet. The last-mentioned is needed to read the many Western words in advertising, or to decipher the functions of tape recorders, cameras, etc., which are produced for the world market.

Japanese can also be represented quite adequately in the Western alphabet alone (as is being done in this book, which employs one of the many possible systems of transcription). However, there are two major reasons why the old system is being retained:

(a) There are countless words (mostly Chinese loan words), which are pronounced exactly the same, for example **toku**, which can mean a profit, a virtue, to dissolve, to untie, to explain, to preach, as well as swiftly. Apart from context, the only way to differentiate between them is each one's different **kanji**.

(b) Once learned (and Japanese school children are said to take the equivalent of two years more than Western children to be able to read fluently) **kanji** exert a powerful attraction on the reader with their intrinsic beauty and direct appeal (always assuming that one has learned their meaning!). It is rather like suddenly seeing two flags: one with the direct picture of hammer and sickle on it, and the other one only with the writing (alphabetic or in **kana**): 'Hammer and Sickle'!

For this reason the present system, in spite of post-war attempts to abolish it, is here to stay.

Traditionally, Japanese (like Chinese) is written in vertical columns, starting at the top right and ending at the bottom left. Thus many Japanese books start on the page where Western books end. However, many books and articles – especially technical writings – are also written in the Western way, from left to right, and from top to bottom. Newspapers and magazines, as well as outdoor signs etc., mix these two ways to create exciting layouts.

wrong machigatta

Y

yawn (*verb*) akubi o suru /akubi o shimas/

year toshi
    this year kotoshi
    next year rainen
    last year kyonen
    every year mainen
    five years go-nen
    five years old go-sai
    See DATES

yellow ki-iro

Yen en

yes hai, e

YES

Yes can be translated in several different ways: **hai, e, ē, ha, un** or even a phrase like **sō des**.

There are two pitfalls to bear in mind. One is purely linguistic and arises in answering negative questions:

aren't there any?	**no, there aren't**
arimasen ka?	hai, arimasen

Unlike English the Japanese response affirms the correctness of the assumption behind the question (in this case that 'there aren't any'). Here are two more examples:

isn't it open?	**no, it isn't**
aite imasen ka?	hai, aite imasen
didn't you buy it?	**no**
kaimasen deshta ka?	hai

The second point to bear in mind is a common source of misunderstanding. It arises when the Japanese uses **hai** to mean 'yes, I am listening' or 'yes, I have understood'. It does *not* necessarily mean 'yes, I agree' or 'yes, I'll do it'. So don't set too much store by this apparently positive type of response (*see also* NO).

yesterday kinō

yet (*positive*) mō
    (*negative*) mada

have you done it yet? mō dekimashta ka?
the work isn't finished yet shigoto wa mada owatte imasen
not yet mada

you anata *etc.; see* PERSONAL PRONOUNS

young wakai

your anata no *etc.; see* PERSONAL PRONOUNS

yours anata no *etc.; see* PERSONAL PRONOUNS

Z

Zen Buddhism Zen
Zen garden Zen-tei
zero zero
zip (fastener) chakku